THE CHEEKY GUIDE TO OXFORD

The Cheeky Guide To Oxford
Written by David Bramwell
Additional material by Richard Hadfield and Jeremy Plotnikoff

ISBN 0 9536110 5 1

Published in 2003 by
Cheekyguides Ltd
PO Box 243
Brighton, BN1 3XT
www.cheekyguides.com

Comments or suggestions: *david@cheekyguides.com*
Business enquiries: *jeremy@cheekyguides.com*

Acknowledgements
Thanks to Jane, Justyn Time, Bill Heine, Mog, Paul from Undercurrents, Robin Darwall-Smith, everyone at Nightshift, Dr Julia Walworth, the very friendly custodian at Christ Church who told funny stories about Harry Potter, and whose name I've forgotten; Rosie Zaldua-Taylor, and anyone else I met along the way who gave me a good story or two. I apologise in advance for any deviation from what you might have told me. It is the Cheeky Guide after all.
Special thanks to Debs and the Moose for keeping the coffee pot on, and for slapping Jeremy when he really needed it.

Image Usage
Many thanks to all the people that once again submited photos, cartoons and writing for this edition. The image of Jeremy Paxman on Page 132 was used as a parody, and in no way implies that Jeremy Paxman endorses Moya restaurant.

Artwork
Illustrations, cover and maps ably supplied by the hugely talented transsexual midget Lisa Holdcroft. Contact (01273) 705658/ *lisa.holdcroft@ntlworld.com*

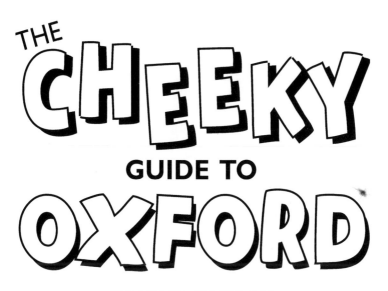

THE CHEEKY
GUIDE TO
OXFORD

SECOND EDITION

Written and researched by David Bramwell

Additional writing and research by Jeremy Plotnikoff and Richard Hadfield

Illustrations by Lisa Holdcroft

Edited by Brian Mitchell

About the Creators of this Book

David Bramwell

Raised by his adopted parents on a strict diet of herring, David developed into a child prodigy and had already, by the age of four, realised that external forces were at play in the Sooty Show.

He graduated from Christ Church when only nine and went on to become one of the top Mathematics lecturers at the University, despite not having followed the more traditional route of acquiring drink and hygiene problems first.

Disillusionment with vector diagrams and complex matrices soon set in, however, and he quit his job, spending the next few years drifting in and out of employment until finally hitting rock bottom playing the part of a Cyberman in a Doctor Who musical alongside Bonny Langford.

The idea for Cheeky Guides came along at a crucial moment, as hard times, desperation and deteriorating health had brought him dangerously close to accepting a job at the gift shop in the Oxford Story.

Being the principle writer and researcher of the book, David is, of course, the one who gets all the blame if someone isn't happy with their reviews, and only recently one disgruntled restaurateur threatened to 'hunt him down like a pig' for derogatory comments about his Eggs Benedict.

Jeremy Plotnikoff

Part Scottish, part Canadian and built entirely of Lego, Jeremy is easy to spot in the streets of Oxford, owing to his angular red plastic body and large yellow head. For years he baffled scientists with his ability to whistle two-part harmonies at the same time until it was later discovered that someone was hiding in his trousers.

A workaholic, Jeremy regularly toils round the clock, culminating in extensive sleep deprivation, and in the final throws of creating this book, he entered states of consciousness, previously only dreamed of by William Burroughs, in which he became convinced that a herd of giant pandas were throwing Garibaldi biscuits at him, which largely accounts for all the spelling mistakes.

After the success of the first Cheeky Guide, Jeremy abandoned his wife and kids and shacked up with 80s sex-kitten, Linda Lusardi. Although they now live together in a luxury penthouse apartment in Florida, he hasn't forgotten his roots and still pops back to Oxford now and again to pick up his royalties from the book.

Jeremy is responsible for the layout and design of this book as well as fiddling the accounts, lying to publishers and implementing crude torture techniques on any potential competitors. Despite all this, he has a nice smile and is a vegetarian.

Dippy

Handsome, gifted and rich, Dippy is not known for any of these qualities but does, however, have a rare talent for opening beer bottles with his nostrils.

Despite the ridiculous nickname, his friends know him better as the Human Beat-Box. Give Dippy a microphone and he will provide hours of top-class entertainment with just some simple bass and snare sounds, although he has, on occasions, been known to throw in some fancy triplets on the hi-hat to woo the ladies.

Dippy joined the Cheeky team in autumn 2000 after returning from South America, where he had spent nine months in a Colombian prison as part of a work exchange programme.

A bit like Brains from Thunderbirds, Dippy is responsible for 'behind the scenes planning' in the Cheeky Empire and, if we all become millionaires, we'll have him to thank. Having almost single-handedly reviewed the cafes and restaurants for the book as well, Dippy is an expert on where to get the best curry in Oxford, but, as a consequence, is now a bit of a fatty.

He is happiest with a bottle of beer in one hand and a cricket bat in the other, but often gets confused between the two, leading to disastrous consequences. He has lived in Oxford for the last 10 years with his collection of Guinea fowl

and his lovely fiancée, Jane, who he got up the duff whilst researching this current edition.

Whilst reviewing this book we ...

• Witnessed the lone musician at a music evening in a pub pick a fight with a punter claiming- 'You called William the Conqueror's mother a bitch' before he was swiftly ejected.

• Met a girl called Gill in one shop who was on probation for being rude to customers. Having informed gullible Americans that they would need to march up and down to see if they were fit enough to do the walking tours, she would then proceed to measure their strides with a tape before gravely announcing her verdict.

• Encountered a 50-year-old woman in knee-high green wellies, dancing like Bez from the Happy Monday's in an otherwise empty pub.

• Got too scared to meet one Oxford eccentric when it became apparent that the author of this book would have had to match him drink for drink in a whiskey session that would have, no doubt, led to his death.

• Got arrested for driving down Broad Street at 4 in the morning, partly because it was illegal, but, more importantly, because the policeman who had been sitting in his car for 4 hours just wanted someone to talk to. He kept us there for 45 minutes, nattering amiably about nothing in particular, and then fined us £30.

• And Dippy met Paul McCartney.

CONTENTS

A Brief History of Oxford

According to legend it all began with a pious young lady called Frideswide, whose tale rather romantically marks the beginning of the town around the 7th Century and is steeped in mystical and spiritual metaphors, as well as having been embellished for a good 1300 years.

Frideswide is said to have been a beautiful princess who, having reached that certain age, had an eager suitor in the shape of a king (presumably divorced). Desiring only to embrace the spiritual life of a nun, and not wanting to spend her days launching ships and eating gala lunches, Frideswide ran away, first to Binsey wood and then to Oxford. Her regal suitor, having already sent out the wedding invitations and booked the jester, followed hot on her trail, determined to take her by force. As he approached Oxford's city gate, however, he was struck blind. Realising that being pushy early on in a relationship always leads to trouble, the foolish young king got down on his knees and begged the girl's forgiveness, at which point (and with a spot of good old fashioned fairy tale magic) she restored his sight and even got rid of his bald patch.

Frideswide went on to set up Oxford's first nunnery on the sight of Christ Church Cathedral, while the king found a niche in the market for black R'n'B music sung by a white man.

The spiritual tone of the legend of Frideswide however was not ill-founded, for by the 13th Century the college buildings were starting to spring up as seats of learning for monastic scholars and Oxford soon became established as a city of religious teaching. Only through a slow transformation over the centuries did other subjects eventually come to be studied here, and even nowadays Media Studies is still frowned upon by many of the colleges as being too 'satanic'. By the 14th Century, as the colleges grew, relationships between the local people and the students (better known then as Town and Gown) had soured to the point of animosity. Although they seem to tolerate each other nowadays and even occasionally inter-breed, a terrible battle between the two took place on February 10th 1355, memorialised still as St Scholastica's Day.

The story begins in Swindlestock Tavern, an ale house in the city centre, where an argument between a student and the landlord over the quality of a glass of wine led to the former throwing the wine in the latter's face and giving him a deadleg. A fight broke out between them, duly erupting into a full-scale brawl that spread through the pub and out into the streets, with students, townsfolk and the odd tourist all joining in. By the end of the day an uneasy truce between Town and Gown was eventually made and the students thought that that was the end of it.

The next morning, however, many of the townsfolk were still feeling bloodthirsty and so roped in hundreds of other laymen from the surrounding villages to help them. Woefully outnumbered this time, the students that didn't flee the city were systematically massacred and by the end of a two-day battle, over 60 had been killed. The king, having caught wind of what was going on the previous day, had sent orders for the massacre to stop, yet this had fallen on deaf ears. By way of punishment he made the townsfolk pay an annual fine to the University and gave the colleges certain privileges which included the setting up of their own police force and free handguns for the students. The handgun law was finally abandoned in the 1960s when an Oriel student, confused by his new shiny toy, accidentally shot the college gardener, but every year on St Scholastica's Day, the townsfolk of Oxford must still, by law, visit one college and kiss the feet of the first student they see.

Nearly three hundred years later, one of the strangest events in Oxford's history took place when its citizens woke up morning to find that, overnight, their house prices had doubled and a series of trendy taverns had sprung up on the High Street. Rather surprisingly, Oxford had suddenly become the capital of England. This decision had been made by Charles I, who moved his court here for three years to do battle with Cromwell and his parliament during the Civil War. For a while the king and queen moved to Christ Church, but, unused to such poky and cramped conditions, they found themselves forever fighting over the sock drawer and eventually the queen moved into nearby Merton College. For three years the town found itself (willingly or otherwise) aiding Charles' efforts to keep his power in the country.

It didn't go quite to plan, however, and after Charles' head and body parted company, Oxford quickly returned to its former self and plans for a Metro system were quietly dropped.

For the next 300 years the colleges found themselves slowly being encroached upon by the ever-growing city. By the Second World War Oxford was nearly as important for car manufacturing as it was for education, but it was still its beauty and academic reputation that saved it from Hitler's bombs, as he had set his heart on the city as the headquarters for his occupation of England.

Since then the dominance of the University has given way further still to other businesses, including, of course, tourism. This industry has grown to such an alarming extent that in summer, when the streets get too over-crowded, the council arranges for fleets of open-topped buses to collect visitors, who are taken to the old disused prison and made into jam.

Although the University has consistently produced some of the country's best-known politicians, writers and poets, in more recent years the town itself has won renown for producing some world-famous guitar bands, including Supergrass and Radiohead. And for the last 15 years every granny in the country has been glued to the TV to witness the late John Thaw running like the clappers round Oxford, usually in search of a dead body or a kebab. The success of Morse has brought the city a new kind of fame, revealing its lesser known corners and even spawning a new breed of tourist, which has finally led one drinking establishment proudly to erect the plaque: *'Morse has never been filmed here.'*

Filming Inspector Morse on Broad Street

How to get Here

BY CAR

You can get to Oxford from London or from the Midlands via the M40. Get off at Junctions 8 or 9, both of these run into the City Centre. If you're coming from London, once you're off the M25 the drive is about 30-40 minutes, depending on how dilapidated your car is.

BY RAIL

Most rail passengers tend to come via Paddington Station in London. The trains are frequent, but the times change seasonally, so it is always best to call first. Direct trains are available from cities other than London but often you'll end up routed through every town in England, Scotland, and Wales before finally getting there.

National Rail Enquiries
0845 7484950
www.thetrainline.co.uk
www.ticketmaster.co.uk

BY BUS

If you're coming from London, buses for Oxford leave from just outside Victoria Station. There are a few companies that offer this service, the main two being the Oxford Tube and the Oxford Express. The buses leave every 12-15 minutes during daytime hours. The service operates 24-hours a day, but it is best to check times if you are leaving in the small hours.

Oxford Tube
(01865) 772250
www.stagecoach-oxford.co.uk/oxfordtube

Oxford Express
(01865) 785400
www.oxfordbus.co.uk

National Express
(0990) 808080
www.nationalexpress.co.uk

BY TAXI

Only big show-offs do this, but if you really feel that public transport is beneath you, then a taxi from London to Oxford will cost about £75.

BY PLANE

Getting Around

From Gatwick there is a direct bus to Oxford, which takes about two hours. The service runs round the clock from the north and south terminals, and costs around £20-25 for a return. Taxis from Gatwick to Oxford cost £100.

From Heathrow there is a direct bus service which takes about 70 minutes. The service runs round the clock from the Central Bus station at the airport and costs around £15-£20 for an open return.
A taxi from Heathrow to Oxford will cost approximately £60.

BY RIVER

Having two rivers and a canal passing through it means that Oxford is still often reached by boat. Barges, steamboats, canoes and catamarans regularly bring the more adventurous travellers to the city, although parking is becoming an increasing problem and canoe theft is rife. Last year a Cambridge student, blown off course in his punt, was found close to a nervous breakdown having spent two days asking bemused passers-by where to find King's College.

Contentious issues #1: Traffic

To say that Oxford has a traffic problem would be like saying that Pavarotti is a bit portly. This has been a thorn in the side of town planners, councillors, residents and visitors for as long as anyone can care to remember. Oxford just *wasn't* designed for the motorcar. Of course, the obvious solution would be to knock down a few of the colleges and build some more roads to ease congestion, but not everyone seems to be in favour of this. In fact for many years there has been pressure on Christchurch to allow a road through its meadow, but thankfully they're a stubborn lot and haven't given in to such a ludicrous idea.

If you fancy a long tedious conversation with a local, then mention the traffic problem and watch them rant and rave for a good half-hour. A final word of warning; many an Oxonian bus driver's sole purpose in life seems to be to reduce the number of pedestrians as drastically and efficiently as possible, so watch yourself when crossing the roads, especially down at Carfax.

A loophole in Oxford's parking strategy

I shouldn't really tell you this, but just by Magdalen bridge is an old dis-used fountain with a space next to it that neatly fits one car and is free. Wily drivers use it regularly, so they'll probably be annoyed that I've mentioned it, but anyone daft enough to try and park in Oxford needs all the help they can get.

PARKING

If you need to park in town it'll cost you a few quid just for a couple of hours in most places. You can take your chances down St Giles where you'll be in the heart of the town, but it's pretty expensive, usually full and you can't stay that long. Your best bet is to head for the main parking areas in the west near the Station and around Oxpen's road and Norfolk street, which will still deposit you pretty much in the centre of town. You'll find other carparks:

• Behind the Westgate Centre
• Behind Gloucester Green (via Beaumont Street)
• Behind Tesco's on the Cowley Road

If you are a day visitor to Oxford you could instead use the Park and Ride rather than coming into the City and fighting for Oxford's four parking spaces. You will see signs for the Park and Ride on the ring road at:

• Pear Tree (north) Seven days per week
• Redbridge (south) Seven days per week
• Thornhill (east) Monday – Saturday only
• Seacourt (west) Monday – Saturday only

CAR HIRE

All the main hire companies are represented in Oxford, all are similar in price and their numbers are below. If you have no joy with any of these then look in the Yellow Pages, as there are plenty of others. Hiring a car to visit outside Oxford is a great idea, using it to tour the city is, of course, lunacy.

Hertz
(01865) 319972
Avis
0870 60 60 100 24-hour
Central booking line
Budget
(01865) 724884
Europcar
(01865) 246373
A1 Self Drive
(01865) 436500 from £20 per day

BUSES

The Oxford Bus Company
(01865) 785 400
www.oxfordbus.co.uk

Stagecoach
(01865) 772250
www.stagecoach-oxford.co.uk

The bus service in Oxford is excellent, and so it should be for all the arsing about they have done with the roads. Most journeys around town shouldn't cost over a quid. The buses are frequent and take you most places. The flaw in the system seems to be that you can't get from East to North Oxford without changing in the city centre. The only exceptions are the numbers 7A and number 2, which go all the way from Headington to Kidlington via the Banbury road.

TAXIS

Taxis are numerous and flagging one down in the city centre never seems much of a problem, unless it's 2am and you've got sick down the side of your coat. Ordering a taxi from home seems to be an entirely different situation and on several occasions when I've called one they have been late or just not bothered showing up at all. If you have an important engagement call three companies and pray that at least one will turn up on time.

There are taxi ranks at the Railway Station, St George's Place (Gloucester Green), St Giles, Broad Street and on the High.

001 Cabs (01865) 240000
ABC Taxi (01865) 775577
Ace Cars (01865) 770000
City Taxis (01865) 794000
Euro Taxis (01865) 430430
Radio Taxis (01865) 242424

BICYCLE

At the last count, official figures show that there are now more bicycles in Oxford than people to ride them. This is, of course, the proper way to travel round the city and there are a plethora of bike lanes and streets laden with bike racks for your convenience. Bike rentals are available all over town and most shops will quote you for daily, weekly, monthly or term (12 week) rentals. Deposits are required by all, usually ranging from £50-£100. Make sure that the rental includes lock and lights.

Cycle King
128 – 130 Cowley Road (01865) 728262
£12 p/d, £18 p/w, £35 p/m, £50 per term

Bike Zone
Market Street (01865) 728877
£12 p/d, £20 p/w, £50 per term

Cyclo Analysts
150 Cowley Road (01865) 424444
£12 p/d, £18 p/w, £35 p/m (then £5 for every week extra)

Here There & Everywhere

THE CITY CENTRE

Though a seeming labyrinth of shops, colleges, pubs, restaurants and museums, Oxford city centre is actually very small and compacted into little more than a few dozen or so roads. Not surprising, then, that during the tourist season Oxford becomes ridiculously busy, with crowds of visitors and EF students filling the main thoroughfares in the town and converging around the burger bars to sing their national anthem 'We will rock you.' Meanwhile, college students and locals, exasperated at being asked where the university is, for the fifteenth time by witless tourists, will end up pointing down the Cowley Road or sending them to Freud's.

But, if you're new to Oxford don't worry, all is not lost. The city has so many secrets, beautiful buildings and places of interest that, despite the crowds, it is a pleasure simply to walk around and take it all in. At the turn of every corner you can stumble across anything from a museum of shrunken heads to a meadow of cows. There are towers to climb, theatres to visit, galleries to see, parks, gardens and colleges to walk around, and plenty of quiet areas like Merton and Holywell Street where you can get a real taste of the old city.

The Bridge of Sighs

And **should** you find yourself being treated with haughty indifference by locals or students, rest assured that the vast majority of Oxonians share your ignorance of the city. While most residents really don't know one college from the next, if you stopped and asked any student on Catte Street to point out the Spoon Museum, chances are half of them wouldn't know where it was.

With the exception of some of the tackier tourist experiences, there is a surprising discretion surrounding many of the places of interest in the city centre. The colleges only open their gates to the public at select times (and some not at all), while many of the museums and other buildings do very little in the way of making their presence felt. Without guidebook or insider knowledge, many of Oxford's best features could go unnoticed by someone new to the city. But it is precisely this discretion that has saved Oxford from becoming swallowed up entirely by the tourist industry. Despite the visitors, life goes on,

even if yet another dozy American has just stopped someone to ask where the campus is.

BROAD STREET

No other street in Oxford manages to capture so much of the city's character as Broad Street. This short stretch is home to Trinity and Balliol College, Blackwell's, tourist shops, museums, a couple of good pubs, the Sheldonian theatre and the Bodleian Library. Walk down Broad Street on a typical day and you'll see tourists and students milling in and out of the colleges, while just over the road the evil presence of a waxwork dummy college professor lures unwitting visitors into the Oxford Story for a truly forgettable experience.

In the centre of Broad Street lies a cross marking the spot where three Protestant martyrs were burned alive in the 1550s, while further down near the King's Arms you'll find the beautiful presence of the Sheldonian theatre with its carved heads keeping a watchful eye. Hang around here long enough and chances are you'll end up in somebody's holiday snaps.

THE HIGH STREET (THE HIGH)

Stretching from Carfax Tower all the way down to the Cherwell by Magdalen Bridge, The High has been the main artery of Oxford since records began. Charity shops, clothes shops, posh hotels, restaurants and colleges are all squeezed together along it, while tucked away near Carfax Tower at the top lies the covered market; a maze of butchers, fruit and veg sellers, clothes retailers and coffee shops. This market once took pride of place outside on The High up until the 1760s, when, to make the road safer and less congested, it was moved inside. Even back then it seems that traffic on the High Street was a bone of contention.

On May Morning The High is a scene of carnage and chaos as the whole of the town gets up at 5am and tries to squeeze down it to hear the choir sing from the top of Magdalen Tower. Then by about 7am they naturally feel like a pint or three and the pubs open their doors to an onslaught of boozers, happy in the knowledge that last orders is 16 hours away.

With six colleges directly on the High Street and a further nine clustered close by, this is one of the most important streets in the town for the students and in May and June you'll see them dressed in their official gowns coming here for exams. After their final paper the students celebrate by drinking champagne and throwing things at each other. It's amusing to watch, but best to stand at a discreet distance lest you get caught in the crossfire.

Like many other streets in Oxford, The High has plenty of interesting gargoyles, but its strangest must be the one tucked away high up in the corner of Brasenose College, facing St Mary's

Australian students go in search of Cowley beach

Church and opposite Oriel Street. Amongst the grotesque figures and weird creatures is a little man who appears to be squatting down about to evacuate his bowels. He is in fact doing just that. The gargoyle is a cruel caricature of the foremen in charge of the building site here back in 1886. The masons, who worked on this part of Brasenose, hated him so much that this was their revenge.

MERTON STREET

Step off The High down one of its many side streets opposite the Covered Market and you will find yourself in one of the most beautiful parts of Oxford. Merton Street has remained relatively unspoiled for centuries owing to the fact that it still has no shops to lure locals, few cars to pollute it, and its main inhabitants are students. Not only is this wide, dreamy cobbled street composed exclusively of beautiful architecture, but pass down it and you'll get occasional scintillating glimpses of Christ Church meadow which can be reached from Merton Grove.

Merton Street is also home to England's second oldest tennis court, and was used by Charles I in the 1640s when he narrowly lost to Cromwell (5 sets to 7).

One of the lanes that connect Merton Street with the High used to have the rather splendid title of 'Grope Cunt Lane', having earned its name from being a popular spot for 'ladies of the night' to congregate. The name was toned down later to Grope Street, which still caused some hilarity, so it was tamed further still to Grove Street. Finally by some spectacularly surreal leap of the imagination, the council changed it to Magpie Lane.

ST GILES

This wide road begins just by the Ashmolean Museum, eventually splitting into the Woodstock and Banbury Road. Its most recognised feature is the Martyrs Memorial which, like Carfax Tower, is a useful reference point and any time of day and night will be swarming with foreign visitors or EF students waiting for their guide to show up and take them all to McDonalds.

Although the memorial is a shrine to the three Protestant who were burned at the stake in Broad Street, one summer a group of cheeky students doing tour guides managed to convince the tourists that it was the remains of a sunken church from when Oxford suffered an earthquake.

Continue down St Giles and, on your right, you'll pass St John's College with its huge gardens. Further still lie two of Oxfords most celebrated pubs – The Lamb and Flag and Eagle and Child – facing each other across this busy road and waiting for you with open arms.

BULWARK'S LANE

Connecting St Ebbe's to George Street this little known alleyway is well worth seeking out, as it seems to have been all but forgotten by the town's inhabitants. Even at weekends you can follow its windy cobbled path and barely see a soul.

Not only does it make a great alternative to battling through Cornmarket, but, with its high stone walls and old gaslights you might feel that by some strange magic you've been transported into some Sherlock Holmes caper, rather than just out shopping for some new pants.

GEORGE STREET

With its theatres, cinemas, restaurants, chain pubs and clubs, you might be led into thinking that this is Oxford's answer to the West End. Well maybe it is, but, with the exception of the Apollo theatre it could also pass for Doncaster High Street. You will not find the true spirit of Oxford down George Street, but you might find a Pizza Hut, some crap pubs, hen and stag parties, and, at night-time, if you're lucky, get to see a fight.

JERICHO

Tucked away from the main tourist attractions, Jericho is an area of Oxford that doesn't suffer the usual hoards of visitors, yet has something to offer, and is unusual enough to have earned itself a slightly bohemian reputation.

Its name may have derived from its original remoteness from the city, though some claim it is from the Jericho Gardens, which once stood west of the infirmary. Others still believe it is named after the 'Jerry Builders' who constructed the houses here, which of course begs the question – 'what is a Jerry Builder in the first place?'

To get a good feel for the area, take a walk down Walton Street, where you'll find cocktail bars, an art-house cinema and the odd shop (notably Jericho Books). Jericho's two most impressive buildings can be found down Walton Street too. The Oxford University Press looks more grandiose than a few colleges I could mention, while Freud's, a popular place for cocktails and food, looks like a cross between the Acropolis and a garden shed.

Round the corner from Freud's lies Little Clarendon Street, where suddenly Oxford turns all Mediterranean, with many of its cafes spilling out onto the streets in summer, while at the top George and Davis' ice-cream parlour serves every flavour you can think of, from mango to chicken and chips.

If you fancy escaping from it all however, take one of the slip roads past the Oxford University Press building and you'll find yourself down by the Oxford canal (or, if it's wet and slippy, possibly in it). Here you can meet Oxford's barge community –

you can't miss them, they all sport wellies and beards – and either wander along the path back into town, or lose yourself out towards Banbury.

The Jericho Tavern

Through its heydey in the Eighties and early Nineties this legendary venue was the very nerve-centre of Oxford's music scene and host to many hundreds of bands. Some, like Supergrass, went on to play in huge venues, others, like the Nicotines, are dead and buried. Others still, such as Arthur Turner's Lovechild, soldiered on for something like 15 years despite frequent local petitions to the contrary. Although the venue's demise and tragic conversion to the Scream sent the bands and musicians off to Cowley Road, the old room above the pub is still there and may yet be home again some day to a new batch of Radiohead wannabees.

The Cowley road toilets - now a grade II listed building

THE COWLEY ROAD

'It's probably the criminal capital of England, but you can get a good curry there.' Cowley Road resident

Just past Magdalen Bridge, and sitting between Iffley Road and St Clement's, lies Oxford's most improbable street. Something of the black sheep of the family, Cowley Road may be dirty and ugly compared to the rest of Oxford, but its diversity and spirit make it very much the cosmopolitan hub of the city.

A walk up Cowley Road and Oxford suddenly transforms into a mix of curry houses, health food stores, halal meat shops, bizarre clothes shops, squats, sex shops, trendy pubs, health clinics and Fred's Discount Store which, until a few years ago, included cheap erotic underwear in its range of 'basic household utilities'.

At night Cowley Road thrives. Together with its ever-burgeoning pub scene a couple of the city's more credible clubs are located here too;

the Zodiac and Bullingdon Arms. Both have played pivotal roles in the city's music scene, so it's no surprise that all of Oxford's big name bands have lived in the Cowley Road area at some point in their careers, and the likes of Mark Gardner (Ride) and Danny (Supergrass) can still be spotted around. Even Radiohead all lived together at 5 Ridgefield Road back in 1991 to focus on their song-writing.

Keeping on the band theme for a moment, Cowley Road has even been immortalised in the Supergrass song 'The Strange Ones' as, notoriously, it is home to many of Oxford's drunks, druggies, down-and-outs and eccentrics. Walk down the street any time of day or night and, as like as not, you'll be nearly knocked over as a man hurtles by in a Tesco's shopping trolley, a shady individual tries to and sell you an Oxo cube masquerading as dope, and a Scotsman with a bone through his nose accosts you for 50p and a fag. Stories about this place and its peculiar and often disturbed inhabitants are numerous but rarely exaggerated.

A friend of mine tells of her first day in Oxford when, taking a stroll down the Cowley Road, she was surprised to see a barefooted man walk past her talking loudly to himself and wearing what appeared to be a carpet. Moments later, a woman carrying a plank of wood came running up the street shouting – 'Bob, Bob, Bob!!!'

She finally met up with Bob, who was an old drunk guy in a wheelchair, and, on reaching him, stood there panting for a few seconds. Then, having got her breath back, she started hitting him repeatedly over the head with the plank of wood…

I too remember that in the summer I came to live here, a man appeared on the corner of Magdalen Road sitting in a plush velvet chair with another empty chair beside him. After a couple of days of his continued presence I plucked up the courage to ask him what he was doing. *'Street philosophy my friend....'* he said in a thick, sad, Eastern European accent, and beckoned me to sit in the chair next to him.
'……for only 50p I will tell you why your life is a string of meaningless episodes of suffering.'

Although I declined his kind offer, I had been inaugurated into the Cowley Road.

Why is Cowley Road so weird, what is the magic triangle and where can I buy Mr. T slippers?

The area's full correct name of Temple Cowley has led some occultists to conclude that it might once have been owned by the mystical sect of the Knights Templar, thus making the land holy, blessed and magical, which, with all those kebab shops, it clearly isn't. New Age legend also holds that powerful ley-lines run down the

Cowley and Iffley Roads (hence the names Cow-ley and Iff-ley), converging at the sweet counter of Bottom's Up by Magdalen Bridge. This may help explain why Cowley Road is unusual, but fails to explain why Iffley road is so dull in comparison. Live in this area for more than a year, the legend continues, and everyone you come to know will live within it too, your love-life will blossom here, you won't be able to leave for less than 5 years and you will, at some point in your life (regardless of your gender) grow a goatee beard.

The Cowley triangle is capped by Magdalen Road, which is also a spiritual mecca in its own right. Not only is it home to the Inner Bookshop and Magic Café (the focal point of Oxford's hippie and occultist community), but you'll also find a Buddhist temple, a theatre, sharks and piranhas at the Goldfish Bowl and one of my favourite places – Silvester's. Not really existing in the universe as we know it, Sylvester's is a cross between Dr Who's Tardis and the local shop from the 'League of Gentlemen', and seems to stock everything the imagination could conjure up, from Roland Rat tea towels to artificial moss.

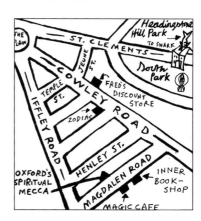

Cowley Rhododendrums

Number 30 Henley Street

Although its heyday has been and gone and it's all a bit run-down nowadays, this garden is still an unnerving spectacle to behold. A breezeblock fortress with a doll's head in one of the turrets sits among other such bizarre items, while half-hidden behind the ivy (that threatens to topple the house) sits a two-foot high shrine with a figure inside. Elsewhere in the ivy, an over-sized owl stares down into the pond that once lit up. Very David Lynch, very scary. Visit at night. Alone.

Number 43 Magdalen Road

A bizarre cross between an Amazonian rainforest and a junkyard for 'Toys-R-Us'. Look for the weird shrine near the front door, dead balloons hanging on the washing line, and the rotting remains of a Welsh flag. Inside is even better, and guided tours might be on the agenda next year.

A typical Cowley Road resident

HEADINGTON

Follow St Clement's and Headington Road up the hill and you'll eventually find this small residential area. Though once the home to writer J.R.R. Tolkien and crooked businessman Robert Maxwell, its most famous and eccentric resident can still be found here; a large fibre-glass shark (crashing into the roof of a residential house on New High Street).

If you do find yourself in the area with time to kill, both Bury Knowle Park (just after the lights) and the old village can be very pleasant for a wander round while Café Noir offers excellent French cuisine.

Bargain hunters, however, may drool at the knowledge that Headington has Oxford's greatest concentration of charity shops (there are at least six or seven of them all close together) and may well wish to spend a full day here stocking up on 'It Shouldn't Happen to a Vet' books, incomplete jigsaws and Herb Alpert records.

PARKS AND GARDENS

Compared to most cities, Oxford has an enviable selection of parks and gardens. You can be almost anywhere in the city and a vast meadow and riverside walk is waiting just around the corner to take you away from the traffic and crowds. Add to that the lawns and gardens of all the different colleges and it's easy to see why Oxford is cherished for its greenery.

Christ Church Meadow

Open 7am-dusk
Entered off St Aldate's through
the War Memorial Gardens

This beautiful meadow lying in the very heart of Oxford is a haven from the noise of the city and home to a rather unlikely herd of longhaired cows which have grazed here for centuries. Pass through the war memorial, and the central pathway (known as Broad Walk) will take you right up to the river where the back of the Botanic Gardens, St Hilda's and the top of Magdalen Tower can all be seen. Take the path round to the right and you can follow the river on its winding trail away from town. Parallel to Broad Walk, and flanking the back of Christ Church and Merton College, is the pathway known as Dead Man's Walk. This was the original path trod by Oxford's Jewish community many centuries ago (to carry their dead from the nearby synagogue to the Jewish burial ground now the location of the Botanical Gardens).

Anti-Semitism was the reason for this special route, as Jews were not permitted to take their dead through the city-centre. Nowadays it is steeped in legends and ghost stories, which probably sprang more from its evocative name than anything else.

South Park

Found at the top of St Clement's
on the right

Renowned for its majestic view of the dreamy spires (if you ignore the cranes and telegraph wires in the background), this park is found just up from St Clement's and creeps up the hill all the way to Brooke's University. It has plenty of space for football matches (including a few marked pitches), a few good climbing trees, and a rather dilapidated fitness trail in the top corner. Throughout May to August it is host to the council organised Party in the Park events, when it is transformed with firework displays, bands, fairground rides and lantern processions. And after the success of the Radiohead concert here in 2001, we may well be seeing more big names here in the future.

Headington Hill Park

Halfway up Headington Road on the
opposite side of the road to South Park

While its neighbour, South Park, is little more than a big field for football games, Headington Hill is the perfect park for a romantic stroll, or some quiet introspection. Especially beautiful in spring when the trees blossom, huge carpets of daisies cover the ground and a host of friendly squirrels turn it all into a Walt Disney cartoon.

Happy cacti in the Botanic Gardens

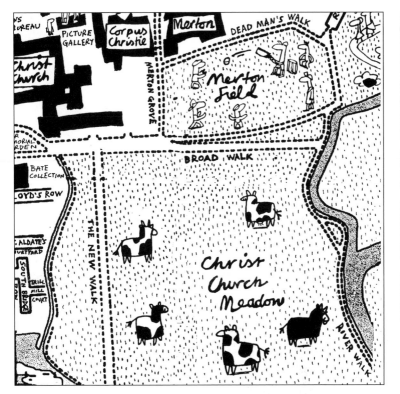

University Parks

Parks Road
Open 8am to dusk

Centrally located and partly encircled
by university buildings, this 100-acre
park lives up to its name, being a
popular spot for student joggers and
the University Cricket Team to
practice, while the more sensible
students can be found idling here over
a bottle of Pimms.

Despite its popularly, it is still
possible to lose yourself in the Park
grounds. Walk all the way to the back
and the orderly array of mown lawns,
flower beds and fir trees give way to a
wild meadow beside the river
Cherwell, offering the opportunity for
an idyllic riverside walk.

The Botanic Gardens

By Magdalen Bridge on the High Street
(01865) 286690 Open 9am-5pm
April-Sept, 9am-4.30pm Oct-March,
Greenhouses open from 10am

Built on the site of the old Jewish
burial ground, the Botanic Gardens
were originally set up for the
cultivation of medicinal herbs in the
17th Century, but have since grown to
become one of the country's most
diverse collection of plants.

As with so many of Oxford's best
features these gardens are all too easy
to miss (being, as they are, set back
from the busy High Street and badly
signposted), but are a really worth
making an effort to visit, not least for
their glasshouses. As one of its staff

said to me: *'Plunge in on a cold winter's day and it's like stepping into another world.'*

Rather than tomatoes and runner beans, you'll find all sorts of exotic plants here, with each 'greenhouse' having its own species and its own unique smell. Look out for the giant oil palm and the cacti room full of enormous prickly characters and carnivorous plants. The greenhouse with the pond and big lily pads also has these tiny fish that nibble your fingernails when you put your hands in the water (though they didn't seem that interested last time I was here).

Meanwhile, around the gardens themselves fans of Phillip Pullman's 'His Dark Materials' trilogy may wish to seek out the seat under the Cornus Mas in the furthest corner by the river (the more sentimental have even been known to leave love-hearts there for Tom and Lyra), while Tolkien fans can be satisfied by looking for the big black pine tree, said to be the author's favourite spot in Oxford.

Another curious feature is the 'Black Border', located outside the orchids greenhouse and facing the river. This strange collection of different black plants looks altogether alien amongst all the greenery of the garden.

And finally don't miss the 'midgets' maze' at the front of the building just before you re-join the High Street. Legend has it that this feature was constructed in the late 18th Century for the dwarf children of the Dean of Magdalen and has been kept in perfect condition ever since their tiny ghosts were spotted playing here over 100 years ago by one of the gardeners.

The gates of Trinity College

Wonderful Things To Do

MUSEUMS

The Ashmolean Museum

Beaumont Street (01865) 278000
www.ashmol.ox.ac.uk
Open Tues-Sat 10am-5pm Sun 2-5pm
Free admission

This beautiful building, reputed to have once been a Roman brothel, is the grand home to a plethora of pots, coins, paintings, statues and jewellery. And while the building itself is a spectacle to behold (both outside and in), the same, however, can't always be said for its exhibits. Presented in an antiquated and dry manner, most artefacts sit lifelessly in glass cabinets or on the wall, and with no interactive facilities and very little in the way of information about them, after a while you might not care less whether the vase you're looking at is Grecian, Ming or Ikea.

To make the most of your visit I recommend talking to the curators, found dotted around the place. This may seem a bit daunting, but, if you feed them a few nibbles (Rich Tea biscuits and Pepperami seem to go down well) they'll tell some good stories about the different items in each room and make your visit *infinitely* more enjoyable. My own personal highlights of the Ashmolean include the Egyptian section on the ground floor, and the Indian gallery, which has an impressive collection of statues of Hindu and Buddhist deities.

On the first and second floor there are plenty of paintings, mainly revolving around the themes of fruit, vegetables, Christianity and dead ducks. One notable highlight, the painting: *'Big nose and shells'* can be found in room 38, and viewed from the special seating area.

As with so many other Oxford attractions, this museum can get a bit packed during the tourist season, so early morning visits are advised. Otherwise, on weekdays you might find yourself surrounded by parties of school children running around doing Harry Potter impressions in the Egyptian and Greek rooms. Weekends, on the other hand, seem especially reserved for visitors who prefer to be engulfed by impenetrable crowds of foreign students sporting novelty sheep rucksacks.

Choose your own nightmare.

Other highlights:

Guy Fawkes' lantern Room 27
The mummified hand Room 28
The Alfred Jewel Leeds Gallery 1st Floor
The Stradivarius Music Room
(Reputed to be the best violin in the world. It is in a protected glass cabinet, but, if you put down a 50p deposit, they'll let you have a go on it)

29

The Theft of the Cézanne

While the dawning of 2000A.D. was predicted as triggering mass cult suicides, the millennium bug and the end of Celine Dion*, the only extraordinary event on New Year's Eve happened right here in Oxford.

In a style straight out of Pink Panther movies, two guys came through the skyline into the Impressionists Gallery and set off smoke bombs. While the guards went to call the fire brigade the thieves helped themselves to the Cézanne painting 'Auvres-sur-Oise'. In the room were other paintings by the likes of Picasso and Monet which mysteriously were left alone. Police figure this to be the work of two men – one a rich art lover and the other a renowned criminal – and have just recently released these crude photo fits.

*She made a pledge on TV to give up singing in the New Year but this seemed to be somewhat akin to Status Quo's farewell tour back in 1986

Bates Collection of Musical Instruments Faculty of Music

St Aldates (01865) 276139
www.ashmol.ox.ac.uk/bcmi-page.html
Open Mon-Fri 2-5pm Sat 10-12pm
during university terms Free admission

From Alpine horns to harpsichords, this is a small but varied collection of Western classical instruments from the last few hundred years. Nothing can be played or touched except the Muselaar (a sort of harpsichord) which, thanks to the over-zealous hands of small children, has missing and out of tune notes, but still makes a gorgeous sound. If you bring kids, get them to look out for Bertie the bat.

Curioxity

Old Fire Station 40 George Street
(01865) 247004 Open weekends, half terms
and school holidays 10am-4pm

Having chosen half term to review this place, I found it hellish, as it was unbearably hot, stuffy and packed with ankle-biters. And they wouldn't even let me smoke in there. But, if you've got kids they'll love the place. It's all hands-on science stuff with two-way mirrors, optical illusions and other gizmos. The price seems a bit steep for what it is but your children will have great fun for an hour. The challenge, as with all kids, is to see how quickly they can break the childproof exhibits.

A cheeky tale

The last time I was in the Ashmoleon with co-writer Dippy, we were passing one of the old curators engrossed in her crossword when Dippy chose that moment to drop a silent stinker. Without even looking up she calmly pulled out a can of air freshener from her bag, sprayed it in Dippy's direction and immediately returned to her crossword, not a flicker of emotion on her face. A true professional.

Tracy Emin's wobbly pier at MOMA

Museum of Modern Art (MOMA)

30 Pembroke Street (01865) 7227733
www.modernartoxford.org.uk
Recorded information line (01865) 813830
Gallery Hours: Tues-Sun 10am-5pm, Sun
12pm-5pm, closed Mondays
Free admission and disabled access

This recently refurbished gallery space has, in the past, mounted exhibitions by everyone from Yoko Ono to Tracy Emin, and is an excellent space for allowing its exhibits to 'breathe'. And, when you're through with analysing the latest existential, contextual post-modern display, there's a café downstairs where you can thumb through old copies of 'Hello'.

Oxford University Press Museum

Great Clarendon Street, Jericho
30 minutes tour arranged by appointment
only, up to groups of 4 between 10am and
4pm and last about. To book a tour, call
(01865) 353527 and make sure to give them
at least 24 hours notice.

Modelled on the arch of Constantine, the Oxford University Press building in Jericho is far more impressive than some of the University buildings I could mention. The museum is housed in one of the rooms here and I must admit, after a brief look at the place I thought I was going to find it pretty dull. But Jennifer who showed me round made me glad I'd visited as she told a few good stories about the place and made it all pretty interesting.

The exhibits are kept in one room and you're basically taken on a half-hour tour with anecdotes about each, from early printing devices right up to the Biggles books.

Once past the 1920s hot metal printing photo (look for Douglas Hurd sat in the centre), the story becomes particularly interesting with the introduction of a character called

James Murray. This heavily bearded brain-box, who looked like Granddad from Only Fools and Horses, decided once and for all to fulfil his childhood dream and compile a dictionary in his shed with the help of, amongst other people, convicted murderer Dr Minor. The story, I believe, is being made into a feature film (possible entitled The Professor and the Madman) so I won't spoil the plot but, needless to say, there's a happy ending, as the Oxford English Dictionary is now *the* definitive dictionary worldwide.

If you want to do your bit for the development of the English language, find a new word that isn't in the dictionary, send 4 examples of it in print to these guys, and it should appear in the next update.

Online submission form www.oed.com

The Real Tennis Courts
Merton Street
Admission 50p

Tennis enthusiasts might be interested to know that this is one of only a handful of 17th Century tennis courts in existence, decorated in its original colours of red and black, and still in use. In fact Charles I used these courts to exercise in during the siege of Oxford in the 1640s, though nowadays they seem to be mainly occupied by the kind of men who wear cricket jumpers and still put Bryl cream in their hair. To find the courts, wander halfway down the cobbled part of Merton Street and you should notice the tennis shop on the side of the road closest to the High Street. If you're not a sports fanatic, you might find your 50p better spent elsewhere.

Sporting the latest in dinosaur fashion

The University Museum of Natural History

Parks Road (opposite Keble College)
(01865) 270949 www.ashmol.ox.ac.uk/oum
Open Mon-Sat 12pm-5pm
Admission free

This unassuming museum, found next to University Parks, is like some great adventurer sat by the fire with his pipe and slippers who welcomes you in and waves around in an ambiguous way saying – 'Oh it's nothing really, just a little something I collected when I was in Peru...' before returning to his Sunday crossword.

But don't be put off by its modesty. You'll realise how beautiful this building is from the moment you enter, (well after you've got used to the smell of mothballs anyway), with its dazzling array of zoological and geological exhibits, swimming in light from the high glass ceiling.

The museum is particularly fascinating for children, filled as it is with skeletons, stuffed animals, minerals and dinosaur footprints; in fact, the only things living in here are a colony of bees half way up the stairs and one or two of the curators.

As well as a fascinating and well-presented selection of natural history they also have various temporary photographic exhibitions on display, all of which have been fantastic.

After you've finished marvelling at it all and found Lewis Carroll's dodo and the meteorite, take the stairs up to the balcony and you'll be rewarded with a great view of the building, as well as being scrutinised by half of the UK's bird population from behind glass cases. Look out also for the sun, moon and earth up there. And then, just when you think you're done, there's the Pitt River's Museum at the back to visit.

The Great Darwinian Debate of 1860

The University Museum is well known for having housed the legendary Darwinian debate that romantic scientists (if such things exists) hold as a moment of great triumph over Christianity.

The story goes that, in the library, many eminent men were present, including scientist; T.H. Huxley, and William Wilberforce, the bishop of Oxford.

As the debate got more heated, the Bishop finally stood up and said: *'So tell me Mr Huxley, is it your grandfather's or grandmother's side which is descended from a monkey?'* Amid laughter, Huxley instantly replied: *'I'd rather be descended from a monkey than from a bishop like Wilberforce.'*

What we learn from this however is not that science triumphed over religion but that even the most intelligent people in the heat of a discussion will resort to arguments like *'my dad's better than your dad.'*

33

Science Museum

Broad Street (next to the Sheldonian)
(01865) 277280
www.mhs.ox.ac.uk
Open 12pm-4pm Tues-Sat, 2pm-5pm Sun
Free admission

Built in 1683, this happens to be the world's oldest surviving purpose-built museum, though has only been the Science Museum since 1924, as before it was the original home of the Ashmolean.

As with the Pitt Rivers, this is a museum to intrigue even the sulkiest teenager, as the exhibits here really are quite magical. Housing three floors of fascinating scientific artefacts relating to such subjects as Astronomy, Time-keeping and Alchemy, this place is a delight for lovers of curious gadgets.

On the top floor you'll find such items as Cardinal Wolsey's sundial, a French 100 degree right angle and 20 hour clock (from when Napoleon had a go at turning everything decimal), Babbage's Difference Engine, an alethiometer, and the first ever white sliced loaf. Both ground and top floors also contain some very striking examples of Astrolabes, though even

after reading the information on them and having a hastily improvised explanation from one of the curators, I'm still not sure I understand how they work.

The trip from top floor to basement is a mini Harry Potter adventure as one descends an ornate and ancient staircase, past a low-hung chandelier, into the gloomy stone crypt; home to the museum's original Hammer House of Horror style chemical laboratory, old alchemical instruments and some pretty horrific looking surgical instruments. Look out also for the rather strange 'Experimental Cabinet', with its tiny grotesque figurines suspended on wires and used to demonstrate conductivity (though we'd be here all day if I tried to explain exactly how). The more observant visitor should even spot Einstein's blackboard, high up on the wall. This was presented to the museum in 1931 after Einstein came to Oxford to challenge its head of Physics to a particularly tricky game of hangman.

(For other museums see 'Weird things to do' section.)

St Mary's Tower

High Street
Admission £1.60 adults

While the final ascent up an impossibly narrow spiral staircase is not for the faint-hearted, this is definitely the best of the 'stunning views of Oxford' on offer. Not only are the panoramic sights magnificent, this is also the highest you can get in Oxford without parting with £16 quid on the Cowley Road. The view takes in the four corners of Oxford, most notably looking down over the Radcliffe Camera and the mysteriously quiet All Souls College, as well as Brasenose, Lincoln and Exeter.

Try your best to visit off-season, or, if you can't, first thing in the morning, as waiting half an hour in the heat for a large group of Japanese tourists to descend the staircase may well taint your experience.

And, incidentally, just because there is lots of graffiti up there doesn't mean that it's an open invitation for all and sundry to join in.

A Brief History

The church and its tower date back as far as the 14th Century when this unassuming little place was actually at the very centre of student life. Renowned men of Oxford, such as John Radcliffe and John Wesley, are buried here, and the church has been used for everything from examinations, ceremonies and lectures to executions. Being an expert in Baroque architecture, I couldn't let you visit St Mary's without asking you to look out for the south porch of the church. With its impressive lattice columns modelled on St Peters in Rome, it cuts a fine figure on the High Street.

I remember being there one summer and watching incredulously as a respectable looking Italian man in his late fifties, accompanied by his equally well-groomed wife, pulled a pen out of his pocket, nonchalantly scribbled his nameon the wall and then resumed licking his ice cream.

oohh… *…ahhhh…*

The four stunning views of Oxford from Carfax Tower

…mmm… *…eurgh.*

Carfax Tower

Top of the High Street
Open April 1st - end of October
10am-5.30pm Winter arrangements
changeable Adult £1.20 Child 60p
No under 5s (01865) 252761
www.oxford.gov.uk for more details

This tower is the only remains of a 13th Century medieval church, and the name Carfax comes from the Latin- *'Quadri furcus'*, an ancient four mushrooms pizza topping, and a reference to the shape of the church's four enormous bells. For your money you get to climb the 99 steps of the tight winding spiral staircase for the awesome view of the town. Once at the top make sure to take a look through the free telescope.

Although it says 20p, it's actually been broken for years, and, despite being really tricky to get a coin in, still manages to take about £200 a year.

When you've finished enjoying the views and taken far too many photos, look out for Oxford's most surreal graffiti – *'we bow to Kaboola, god of cheese'*. I've no idea what that's all about.

And, finally, on the way down look for the crucified rabbit in the glass cabinet.

During high season it can be ridiculously busy and uncomfortably claustrophobic. To avoid the crowds come **very** early in the morning.

A Brief History

By 1032, St Martin's Church (now Carfax) stood at the town centre's main crossroad and entered history as the spot where the infamous "Town and Gown" riots took place in 1355.

A lesser-known fact about Carfax Tower is the existence of a child's grave on the way in just under the chair on the left. In fact, the old graveyard of this church still lies below the café next door, but, for some reason, they've chosen not to broadcast the fact.

OTHER INTERESTING BUILDINGS

The Sheldonian Theatre
Broad Street
Open 10-12.30pm 2-4pm Admission £1.50

Built in the late 1600s by Sir Christopher Wren, the Sheldonian's name and design derive from Roman origins and for many centuries it was used principally for ceremonial purposes. Nowadays it is still used by the universities for degree-giving ceremonies but is used much more for music events. You won't see Oasis in here, but everything from Beethoven to Cleo Lane, *'as long as they're in keeping with the building and don't wreck it'*. For the tour you get to climb to the cupola for a panoramic view of Oxford, which gives a good opportunity for some gargoyle spotting.

Personally, I'd recommend saving your money and experiencing the Sheldonian properly by coming to a concert, but, if that's not possible, it's worth a visit, especially if you're around in June for Encaenia. This is the one time when all the top nobs from the universities get dressed up and parade through the town to the theatre where they deliver honorary degrees to anyone with a fat enough chequebook.

Life for the students at Oxford begins and ends at the Sheldonian Theatre. In the second week of the first term everyone dresses up in Sub Fusc* and then after a 10 minute speech in Latin (which no-one understands) they are official students of Oxford, and everyone celebrates with a glass of fizzy pop. Life at the University ends with Matriculation (the graduation ceremony), although this has to be booked by each student separately and I have heard nightmare tales of students waiting up to four years to graduate.

The Radcliffe Camera
Radcliffe Square
No public access

Opened in 1749, this magnificent round library was built as a glorified reading room for students but, over the years, has not only become an extension of the Bodleian Library nearby, but also one of the most photographed buildings in Oxford. Entering, however, is a privilege normally reserved solely for students, so there is little more I can tell you beyond the apocryphal but charming tale of a don from Brasenose who, famously, would get so blind drunk each night he would have to feel his way along the walls of the Camera to get back inside his college. Apparently one time he was so pissed that he staggered across to the building and spent the whole night just going round and round....

The Radcliffe Camera

*The clobber they wear for exams and graduation

WONDERFUL THINGS TO DO

Caudwell's Castle and Folly Bridge Tower

Folly Bridge, St Aldates
No public access

Down on St Aldate's, this unusual building can be found just to the right of Folly Bridge. Built in 1849, this Venetian Palazzo style affair was dreamed up by wealthy eccentric Joshua Caudwell, who delighted in surrounding his home with classical statues and cannons. The whole thing is ridiculously over the top but still much more in keeping with Oxford's architecture than some of the 20th Century monstrosities I could mention.

How Roger saved Oxford's bacon

Folly Bridge Tower is the location of a story about how a couple of centuries ago a bunch of cocky Cambridge students came to Oxford intent on proving once and for all that Cambridge undergraduates were intellectually superior.

On arriving at the tower they called up in Latin, expecting to humiliate the simple custodian they imagined would be working there. But the tower's custodian happened to be none other than one of the 13th century's most famous scholars, Roger Bacon, (doing a bit of part-time work on the side) and he naturally replied in fluent Latin. This was enough to intimidate the Cambridge students. If the keeper of the tower could speak fluent Latin, they figured that the Oxford students would probably have mastered the ability to travel backwards in time and how to make the perfect puff-pastry. The story ends with them fleeing back to Cambridge and to this day bacon is still off the menu in most Cambridge colleges.

The Bridge of Sighs

New college Lane

One of the most famous sights in Oxford, the Bridge of Sighs is, of course, modelled on the famous Venetian bridge that connected to the prison from which Casanova escaped. This one, however, was built in the late 19th Century to connect Hertford College Old Quad with the New Quad and to give its students ease of access between the two. After a survey in 1995 revealed that of all the students in Oxford, Hertford's were *'the most portly'*, it was blocked up as part of the college's efforts to ensure its students got more exercise.

Oxford Castle
New Road. No public access

Built around the time of the Norman Conquest, this hasn't fared well against the ravages of time and nowadays is not so much a building as a grassy knoll. Despite it being officially out of bounds to the public, it is used in winter by snowboarders seeking cheap thrills, and is a popular spot in summer for fornicating students.

The Bodleian Library and Gallery
Old School's Quad (01865) 277000
Open Mon-Sat 9.30pm- 4.45pm
Admission free

Built above the Divinity School, this is one of only three copyright libraries in England, which receive a free copy of every new book published. The Library is part of a confusing cluster of buildings that sit in Old School's Quad opposite the Bridge of Sighs and is open only to students who use it as a reference library. Paid tours are organised a few times a day for visitors and will take you around the Duke Humphrey's Library and Divinity School, although the price is a bit steep and it's not that exciting either. It's better just to wander through here from Radcliffe square or Catte Street and look at the buildings.

Trivia
Students still have to take an oath that they won't take sheep inside the building, while statistics suggest that each book in the Bodleian Library is read approximately once every 16 years.

View into the Old School's Quad

The Ice Rink
Oxpen's Road

Disfigured in his early teens by an experiment with a chemistry set that went tragically wrong, architect Colin Grote perhaps best described his bitter hatred of the world with the design of this building. Despite winning many awards, (in particular the coveted *'Hurray for Grey'* prize in 1968), it still manages to court controversy and in the 1980s incurred the wrath of Prince Charles who, during his famous 'monstrous carbuncle' speech on the state of British architecture, added that the Oxford Ice Rink looked like a *'a corrugated dog turd with tentacles.'* In a nutshell, it's pig ugly.

39

Merton Street

WHERE TO TAKE A GOOD STROLL

City Centre

Your mission, should you accept it, is to find Magpie Lane half way down the High Street. Once down this narrow side street you'll be in one of the most unspoiled parts of Oxford; Merton Street. This long cobbled road is home to a cluster of colleges and despite its beauty, is little travelled by many Oxford residents, as there are no shops down here. But it is precisely the lack of pedestrians and cars that make it all the more magical. Continue until you're back to the High, cross the road and to your left head down Queens Lane; another quiet, timeless street. Make sure to look out for a motley collection of gargoyles staring down at you from the high wall of

New College on your right, then as you pass the bend you'll be rewarded with the Bridge of Sighs. Down the alleyway just before it (once known as Hell Passage), lies the beer-drinkers utopia known as the Turf Tavern. From here most people forget about the walk and concentrate on sampling all the different ales in the pub.

If you make it out of the Turf alive, take a left onto Catte street and you'll pass two of Oxford's most famous buildings, the Bodleian Library and the Radcliffe Camera. To finish your walk in style, take a trip up St Mary's tower at the end of the square for a panoramic view of the city and a chance to get intimate with groups of American tourists in the tight passageways at its top. Back to earth you'll find you're almost exactly where you started, though tired, wiser and possibly a little sozzled.

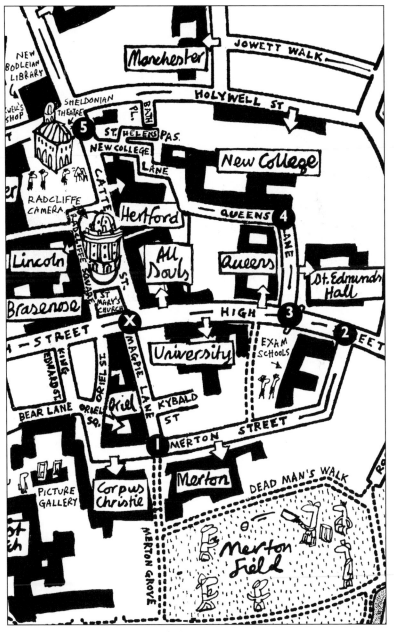

CITY CENTRE WALK

Start at the cross and follow the numbers.

River Walk
St Aldate's

Down St Aldates, past the Head of the River pub you'll find, just after the cruise boats, a path on your left leading to the river. This path meanders its way along the Isis all the way to Donnington Bridge, passing some lovely countryside, the resident swans and the myriad rowing establishments. During term time you might be lucky to catch the University rowing teams out with the coxes, who cycle alongside the rowers shouting insults to spur them on. When you reach Donnington Bridge, take a left and Iffley Road will lead you back into town, or turn right to reach Abingdon Road. Continue under the bridge, however, and you'll reach the Isis Tavern where lunch and a beer await.

A word of warning: if it has rained recently, this can be a relentless nightmare of puddles and mud.

Port Meadow

To find it go down Walton Street past the Phoenix Cinema, turn left at the small roundabout past Lucy (a factory) and you'll find the car-park at the bottom of the road.

Port Meadow is a vast stretch of greenery on the edge of Oxford, used for the Oxford horse races in June, and best loved for the walk to the Perch and Trout public houses a few miles along the river.

To get to the Perch, go straight across the meadow and, once over the bridge, turn right. After passing the boat yard, it is about another twenty minutes walk from here.

For the more adventurous, the Trout is another couple of miles along the river. Not only is it a better pub, but the walk gets pleasanter from here too. Continue and the path will widen out with more meadowland and trees on your left. Once over the lock you're almost there and, if it's after 12pm and the height of summer, you've only a short two-hour wait before you get served.

Canal Walk
Jericho

Starting at the upper end of Hythe Bridge Street and continuing all the way to the bridge on Walton Well Road, this is a twenty-minute stroll along Oxford's canal, taking in the barge community, plenty of greenery, and a few ducks. To know where to leave the trail, look for the red brick bridge (you'll recognise it as the walk tails off with the arrival of an ugly dilapidated building on your right). Turn right at the bridge and you'll be back on Walton Street, where it's only a short stroll into the town centre, though I recommend stopping first at the Jericho café for a bite to eat.

For the more adventurous, the canal walk does continue all the way to Banbury, but it might take you a day or two to get there, so make sure you pack enough provisions.

Iffley Village and Lock

Iffley village, engulfed by the ever-expanding town of Oxford many years ago, and once threatened with being flattened under Stephenson's railway, somehow survived. What's more, it has withstood the ravages of change to remain an attractive and quiet village on the outskirts of Oxford. To get there, follow the Iffley Road from town and once you're past the Donnington Bridge lights, take the second right. From here, cross the small roundabout and you'll find yourself in this village.

Wander along Church Way and you'll pass The Prince of Wales, which is worth noting for one of the best pub lunches in Oxford. On reaching Mill Lane on your right follow this road down to the end, go through the narrow sheltered walkway, and then over the lock. I've done this walk most times of year, from the coldest winter night when your breath hangs frozen in the air, to the warmest summer morning and it always brings a rush of happiness.

Once over Mathematical Bridge, to your left is the meadow supporting one of England's rarest flowers, the Snakeshead Fritillaries, while, to the right, is the path along the lock to the Isis Tavern. If you continue on this path by the river it'll eventually lead you into the heart of the town and, curiously, you'll be at the start of the St Aldate's river walk.

PUNTING

*O*ne of the most wonderfully frustrating activities to undertake in Oxford. Be very careful not to underestimate the complexity of moving a boat between point A & B with a pole. Invariably, you will also visit points D, E and Y, but you will have learned something along the way.

Oxford provides a number of locations to begin your adventure, all of which allow you to explore different parts of the river and also various drinking houses during you trip. Be aware of the long traditions associated with the sport. The most famous is the 'punter's' standing position. In Oxford we stand on the curved, rough end of the punt, while in Cambridge they stand on the smooth, flat end. Weighing up the pros and cons of each, the Oxford method is, of course, by far the most efficient and attractive.

HOW TO PUNT

1) Get onto your boat.
2) Stand on the curved end of the punt.
3) Check there are no splinters along the pole. If there are, remove them and sand down the remaining surface.
4) Never try and get more than five or six people in a punt. Over thirty is really asking for trouble.
5) Look confident and don't slouch.
6) Push away from riverbank.
7) To go forward, keep the pole tight to the boat at a sharp angle facing away from the punt.
8) Raise pole to full extension and drop through hands into water until contact is made with the bottom of river.
9) Use the pole as a rudder to steer out of the way of oncoming vehicles and large ducks (some of which have been measured at two metres in length and have been known to wrestle unwary punters to their watery grave).
10) Remember, you have to get back to where you started, so don't be too ambitious in your journey, London is further than you think.
11) Watch out for bridges as you have a very long pole in your hand and it points straight up in the air.
12) Whatever you do, never hold onto the pole when it gets stuck into the mud. It is better to lose the pole than your hard-earned dignity.

FIGHTING TECHNIQUES

When ramming another punt, aim for the standing punter. The pole can be used to hit the opponent's ankles but remember to keep low at moment of attack.

Do:

1) Bring booze. Pimms and fizzy white wine are very popular.
2) Go when it's sunny.
3) Swing from low branches as you pass beneath them.
4) Be careful of large boats when punting on the Thames.
5) Take water pistols.
6) Take sun tan cream and waterproofs.

Don't:

1) Bring any pets, especially Dulux dogs, large members of the cat family, or horses.
2) Attempt punting when under the influence of strong hallucinogenics.
3) Rock the boat (unless copulating).
4) Bring any high voltage equipment on the punt with you.
5) Drink from the river, unless you collect unusual skin complaints.

PUNTING COMPANIES

Cherwell Boathouse

To find it go along the Banbury Road, right into Bardwell Street and watch out for signs. £8-10 per hour. £40-50 all day. Deposit – one day's hire. Available 10am-7pm. mid March-mid Oct. (01865) 515978

The main advantage of coming here is the lack of powered vehicles on this stretch of the river and the places nearby to eat. Tea Hut, at the boathouse, is an excellent but pricey restaurant, while, about an hour upstream, is the Victoria Arms, which has a docking station, a play area, and is open all day, with pub grub from 12pm-2.30pm. Downstream, the University Parks is excellent for picnics and, a bit further, is Parsons Pleasure, once a nude sunbathing area used by University dons and now a family-friendly picnic area for naturists.

Magdalen Bridge

Old Horse Ford, underneath the bridge. (01865) 202643 £10+ per hour. £25 deposit and ID required.

This place has been operating for over 100 years, and is a great starting point for drifting down past the Botanic Gardens and beyond to Christ Church Meadow. If you continue you can reach the Head of the River pub for refreshments and a chance to be photographed by a party of foreign students. You can also organise chauffeured punts from Magdalen Bridge, it's pretty expensive, but you do get free fizzy white wine.

There are also two more punting spots to be found by to The Head Of The River pub on St Aldate's.

Weird Things To Do

The Pitt Rivers Museum

Behind the Natural History Museum,
Parks Road (01865) 270927
Open 12pm-4.30 pm Mon-Sat,
2pm-4.30pm Sun Admission free
www.prm.ox.ac.uk

If I had to pick my favourite place in Oxford it would be the Pitt River's. This building is nothing less than a dazzling treasure trove of bizarre yet fascinating ethnological curiosities that would be equally at home in Giles' Magic Box* or an Indiana Jones film, as in a museum.

Housed at the back of the University Museum of Natural History, the Pitt River's has three floors of artefacts, all crammed into wonderfully decrepit glass cabinets. What the top floor lacks in interest with its collection of weaponry, the ground and first floor make up, boasting everything from a 40-foot totem pole to shrunken heads, Voodoo dolls and witchcraft charms.

With its gloomy lighting, some corners are so dark that the curators carry torches around to help visitors read the tiny hand-written labels that accompany the artefacts, but, of course, this only adds to the museum's singular charm. Trying to locate things here can also be problematic, for despite the cabinets

being numbered, the figures are so discreet they are almost impossible to find. Spot something really weird and five minutes later you might never be able to find it again.

Many visitors to the museum fail to spot the drawers that sit underneath the display cabinets, which is a shame. There are literally hundreds dotted around the place and, being unlabelled (obviously), you might open one up to find a mummified toad, while in another a severed finger points back at you accusingly.

As you enter on the ground floor you shouldn't have too much difficulty finding the museum's most notorious exhibits, the shrunken heads. This cabinet, 'head-hunter's trophies,' with its gruesome heads, skulls and scalps, is found underneath the boat hanging from the ceiling, and usually has a crowd around it. And while you're there you might like to look for the 'treatment of the dead' cabinet nearby, with its tiny jar – home to a baby foetus.

Down the right-hand wall of the ground floor can be found the mummy with her little toe sticking out from the bandages (said to wiggle on her birthday) and the weird looking 'Nail Man'. Opposite them, the drawers underneath the 'Sympathetic Magic' section contain some of the museum's best-kept secrets. Look in the top middle drawer and you'll find a beeswax voodoo doll with pins in its eyes. Look out also for the Sussex witch, trapped in a bottle, who, if ever released, is said to wreak revenge on the world. I could go on forever but, needless to say, this museum is just terrific; anyone with a love of the darker side of anthropology will not be disappointed. Allow a couple of hours for a good look around and if you're feeling adventurous, seek out Brian or Eric, two of the curators who could take you on a Zulu trail or show you some of the lesser-known exhibits. It may come as no surprise if I tell you that they are suitably as eccentric as their surroundings.

"I'll show you the chains that cannibals once used for dragging dead bodies out of the ground for rituals," said Eric with a wicked grin, last time I was here.

*The Occult Shop in Buffy the Vampire Slayer

Other oddities
(if you can find them)

GROUND FLOOR
Ballerina flies
Made with head and thorax of a large fly (case 145)

The Hawaiian feather coat
Far left-hand corner, look for the curtains and the light switch

Sheep bones floor
Just to the left of the totem pole at floor level of the primitive dwellings cabinet lies a section of a kitchen floor from the house at number 97 St Aldate's, which was made entirely from sheep's bones.

Severed fingers
magic cabinet in the far right corner

Copulating gingerbread dogs
Bottom drawer, second from right, cabinet 17, far right hand corner

The donation box
*Facing you as you enter the ground floor. This houses several weird carved figures (all based on real people, including Mr Rivers himself!), which bow, and whose eyes light up when you put your money in. Even **this** is a bit scary.*

FIRST FLOOR
Trepanned skull
Found amongst the surgical instruments cabinet as featured in Philip Pullman's 'the Subtle Knife'.

Self-torture instruments
Past cabinet 45 on the left-hand wall Open the thickest bottom drawer and inside you'll find a grizzly collection of home torture equipment once used by the Dervishes. One particular object, a spiked ball for insertion and rotation in the eye socket might, however, put you off your dinner for life.

The tiniest doll in the world
In the games cabinet on the right wall Only 1 cm long. And opposite this in the surgical instruments cabinet lies a small box bearing an alarming-looking spiky object and the eye-watering label-'for operations on the penis'

Pitt Rivers Annex

60 Banbury Road (01865) 270927
Viewing by appointment only

While the archaeology section is nothing to get into raptures about, in keeping with the nature of the Pitt Rivers this place has a suitably bizarre but beautiful collection of musical instruments, ranging from Javanese Gamelans and nose flutes to toy telephones, a squeaky frog and an English kettle.

Compared to its big brother, the collection here is slight but in its favour does have a small garden round the back with a music theme where you can see a variety of plants, ranging from campanula to bamboo, all used for making instruments.

Holywell Cemetery

St Cross Road/ Longwall Street

Just beyond the trimmed, orderly façade of the church front lies Holywell Cemetery, an enchanted garden of tumbledown graves and overgrown flora. Having been spared the lawnmower and rake (as a means of providing a secure home for numerous badgers, foxes, toads and birds) this graveyard gets wilder and more mysterious the deeper one ventures into it, as if it is auditioning for a part in some classic children's fairy story. No surprise, therefore, that the author of Wind in the Willows, Kenneth Grahame, should be buried here.

A little more unexpected perhaps is the grave of maverick drama critic Ken Tynan (best-remembered as the first person to say 'fuck' on television in the 1960s, causing untold complaints and widespread panic among the middle classes).

If you're in the area it's a lovely place to come and take a solitary stroll, especially at dusk, when you will not be too surprised to see elves, pixies and Wombles frolicking together in the undergrowth.

The Shark House

New High Street, Headington

This incredible work of art achieved international fame in 1986 when local prankster Bill Heine became a first-time homeowner and asked his friend and sculptor John Buckley: *'what can we do with this house?'*
John's response was to build and install a fibreglass shark crashing into its roof. The day Bill decided to install it, rather unsurprisingly, the police turned up to find out what he was doing.

One resident couldn't afford the real thing...

'Just sticking a shark in my roof,' was his cheeky reply. The police thought about it for a while and then conceded that there was no law against it, and left. Bill woke the next day to find heavy rain swamping his kitchen, an army of council officials standing outside ready to give him a Chinese burn, and Terry Wogan on the phone. It seemed he'd made the news.

In fact, the shark house quickly became recognised all over the world as a unique piece of art, and it was this that partly saved its skin, as Bill had to fight a six-year battle with planners, councillors and other officials over its survival, owing to the fact that he hadn't actually applied for planning permission. The council at least realised that the shark was something worth keeping, but couldn't handle the idea of it sticking out of Bill's roof, and at one time suggested sticking it in a local swimming pool, which, as you can imagine, kind of misses the point.

In the meantime it was attracting more supporters than critics and even had scouts camping on it for 21 hours in 1988. Resident shark supporter and unofficial archivist June Whitehouse once famously said –

'It doesn't smell, it doesn't make a noise and it's not illegally parked, so what's the problem?'

But the battle continued until, finally, it was left in the hands of the (then) secretary of State, Michael Heseltine, who, legend has it, came to Oxford, walked up and down the street several times, and finally declared in a fit of clarity rare for a politician –

*-There **has** to be a place for the strange and downright quirky in our planning regulations.'*

And so finally the shark was safe.

A SPOTTER'S GUIDE
TO OXFORD CELEBRITIES

What better way to spend your afternoon than going all gooey-eyed and weak-kneed at having stumbled across your favourite celebrity? Oxford is home to a motley collection of comedians, musicians and authors, all of whom will be more than delighted to spend their free time autographing your breasts and listening to you misquote their lyrics, prose or catchphrases. I wish you every success with your sleuthing...

ROWAN ATKINSON

The rubbery-faced comedian can occasionally be spotted around town, and has been known to enjoy the odd meal at Gee's restaurant. Like all good comedians he sports an air of melancholy and sobriety, so the best thing to do, if you spot him, is to try and cheer him up with your own Mr Bean impersonation.
30 points

RICHARD BRANSON

The self-made millionaire lives just outside Oxford in Kidlington but often balloons into Cornmarket trying to blag free CDs from his former empire. Notorious for borrowing taxi money and never re-paying it, if you see him walking towards you looking confused and patting his pockets, run away.
20 points

THOM YORKE

As well as popping up at gigs occasionally, the singer of Radiohead is often spotted loitering around the mushroom section of the big Tesco's at the Cowley roundabout. Whether he's seeking solace in the world of edible fungi, or in need of inspiration for a new song, heaven knows. If you do see him, try to avoid fawning, as he has a reputation for being shy and aloof. Instead, just pop a couple of organic button mushrooms into his hand, bow slightly, then walk away.
25 points

COLIN DEXTER

I've no idea what he looks like (except he describes himself as short and bald) and I'm sure you haven't either, but the writer of Inspector Morse is legendary in these parts for taking every opportunity to draw attention to himself, and has even been known to sport a T-shirt with the motto 'Dexter Here' on it. Also been known to talk to himself on buses.

10 points

DR GRAEME GARDEN

The former Goodie can be found some mornings at the train station having a fag or two, probably waiting to pop into London for his millionth appearance on 'I'm Sorry I haven't a Clue.' If you see him, pinch his fags until he reveals the rules for Mornington Crescent.

15 points

JEREMY PAXMAN

Forever being observed wandering around Broad Street, buying books from Blackwell's or having a pint in the White Horse where invariably he'll be practicing his rudeness on students. If you see him tell him his head is shaped like that of horse then run away before he can think of a sarcastic reply.

25 points

If you've been missed out of our spotter's guide and feel that you ought to be included, please write to us finishing the following sentence:

I think I'm famous enough to be in your guide because

....

Please enclose £10 and a signed photo. Appearing on Sixtv or being an extra in Inspector Morse will not suffice.

A SPOTTER'S GUIDE
TO LOCAL ECCENTRICS

BILL HEINE (THE SHARK MAN)

One of the town's more controversial and colourful local characters, Bill is best known for being the owner of the Shark house and for getting up the noses of local councillors and politicians. Unmissable with his white bouffant locks and dashing moustache, the legendary Mr Heine can be found hosting his local lunchtime radio chat show, organising charity events, endlessly campaigning for equal rights for others, or simply out and about making citizen's arrests on crack dealers and baby snatchers. Yet against all odds always managing to keep his hair immaculate. Prankster, spokesman for the needy, or simply an egomaniac with bad taste in facial hair? You decide.

What the locals think of him:

- 'The old ladies love him, he's a local Anne Robinson.'
- 'I don't like his Hollywood tan.'
- 'A generous man who always throws good parties.'
- 'Who?'

Worth 8 points

JUSTYN TIME, OXFORD'S OFFICIAL JESTER (a.k.a. Stripey Joe)

www.stripeyjoe.co.uk • enquiries@stripeyjoe.co.uk

Taught by Timmy Mallett to juggle through the 'power of television', Justyn quickly developed his magic powers to become what he is today – the official Jester of Oxford. An inauguration on January 13th, 2000 saw Justyn taking an oath to 'bring merriment and happiness to the people of Oxford', and he can often be seen around town entertaining people with his juggling, stilt-walking and magic tricks. In fact, Justyn's notoriety and fame has spread so much that a few years back he had to cancel a kids' party at Blackbird Leys after receiving an emergency royal summons to Prince Charles 50th birthday bash. After turning up dressed in full Jester gear, Justin was looked up and down by a bemused Queen and asked - 'So what are you here for??' Doh.

You can find him down the Cowley Road, in the Magic Café, or in just about any pub you care to think of.

Worth 20 points

MAC

Bald and terrifyingly scary, Mac is a long-time music promoter, notorious boozer, and one-time singer with Oxford's most notorious but now-defunct band – Arthur Turner's Lovechild.

If you meet him, be armed with a bottle of whiskey and don't expect to leave his clutches until it's empty. You might have a hangover from hell the next day, but you'll probably also have some great tales to tell the grandchildren.

Worth 10 points, 25 if sober

COLONEL MUSTARD

The Colonel, also known as Captain Tap, is probably Oxford's eldest known busker (there is a record of him in the Domesday Book), and can be found most weekends somewhere around Carfax and Cornmarket doing a spot of 'tap-dancing'. This grizzly old legend, invariably dressed in wild regalia, came second in the 1981 Bognor Regis Opportunity Knocks competition, so give him the respect he's due.

Worth 20 points

COWLEY ROAD POSSE

The Street Cleaner in full Scottish regalia, the guy with a bone through his nose, the Reverend in his dog collar propping up a bar or two – just a few of the fruitier characters you're likely to spot on a typical day's wander up the Cowley Road.

Worth 5 points each

If you've been missed out of our eccentrics guide and feel that you ought to be included, please write to us finishing the following sentence:

I think I'm odd enough to be in your eccentrics guide because...fish fingers...............

...

Yes I'm over 18, live near the Cowley Road, and dress in an alarming fashion.

Cheesy things to do

If you've already succumbed to buying yourself a novelty Oxford teddy bear and University sweatshirt, or had your photo taken outside the Sheldonian, then you might as well go the whole hog. Here's how.

Bus Tour (CitySightseeing Oxford)

Every 15/ 20 minutes (01865) 240105
www.city-sightseeing.com
Admission: £9 Adults, £3 children under 16,
£7 OAP, students and 16-21 year-olds
Highlights include a drive past Park End
Nightclub and Gloucester Green
Bus Station

Join the happy throngs of tourists as they barge and elbow their way to the top for a front seat, leaving you sitting at the back beside a stroppy German teenager with halitosis. For the rather steep fare of £9 you can have someone pointing out the sights of Oxford, which, if you bothered to get off your lazy backside you could walk around and see for free. For more information, contact Tourist Information, or look out for one of their many stops and simply wait for one to turn up.

Note that the tours are multilingual and boast a 'live guide on some buses', which surely implies that on the **other** buses the poor tour guide has passed away and been left there to rot.

The Oxford Story

6 Broad Street (01865) 790055
Open 10am-4.30pm every day
£6.50 adults, £5.50 Concs

Belittled by locals and sneered at by students, this is, however, one of the most entertaining experiences you can have in Oxford if you love kitsch tourist attractions, or have taken enough medication beforehand.

The journey starts with you handing over your well-earned cash to a few weary individuals looking uncomfortable in period costume. From here you will be transported into a 'realistic' common room for a short film, which provides a distinctly unmemorable 'insight' into how students play croquet and wear corduroy jackets in seminars. The pleasant classical music does, however, allow a moment to remove yourself from the video and think about what you'll eat tonight, or if Eastenders will see yet another character die in a tragic scaffolding accident.

Before arriving at one of the world's scariest indoor roller coasters, carefully study the student's room and ask yourself how many students actually have, not one, but, three Barclays Bank posters on the wall? Hmm, couldn't be a spot of subtle advertising, could it?? Whatever happened to Che Guevara, Trainspotting and that girl on the tennis court scratching her bum? And so for the moment of truth. Are you brave enough to ride Oxford's equivalent of the corkscrew? For this achingly slow ghost-train-style ride you sit behind a desk (nice touch) accompanied, by way of headphones, by your host for the journey – either Timmy Mallett or Magnus Magnusson. If you're doing this for the cheese factor, then Mr Mallet is your natural choice, although surprisingly he isn't that irritating. What *is* irritating, though, is that if you're taller than 5 foot 11 inches (my height) the headphone leads are just that little too short, so when Timmy asks you to turn your head to the right to see a waxwork model of Isaac Newton you end up half-strangled.

On your roller-coaster journey you'll find out about lots of people who discovered stuff, kings who wore platform shoes, and how to make a baked Alaska. If you look carefully enough you'll even spot Buddha. What's he doing here???

At the end you can peruse the gift shop, which excels in useless tat. If you are going to subject yourself to this, it's best viewed in mid-winter, when you won't be surrounded by gangs of marauding foreign students.

> In a poll by the Consumers Association, The Oxford Story allegedly came tenth in a survey of tourist places to avoid. It apparently "leaves visitors with a hollow feeling."

Museum of Oxford

Town Hall, St Aldate's (01865) 252761
Open Tues-Fri 10-4.30pm, Sat 10am-5pm,
Sun 12pm-4pm Admission £2/1.50

The kind of place I remember from school trips, with faded cardboard cutouts of Roman soldiers and plastic models of medieval villages. Nothing to get excited about, I'm afraid; it's a kind of a walk-around version of the Oxford Story with more of a slant towards socio-political, rather than academic, history. Highlights include a skeleton, a mammoth's tooth, and a collection of marmalade jars. I'll spare you the lowlights.

Britain's future...

THE
UNIVERSITY

*T*here are 39 colleges dotted around Oxford, each a separate entity, ranging from 50 to over 600 years old. Some are tiny and can be easily missed, like Mansfield College (located in the basement of Marks and Spencers), while others, like Christ Church and Magdalen, are majestic in size, containing parks, huge gardens, and even herds of animals within their grounds.

With the exception of some of the very modern buildings, the ubiquitous design for every college is the quad, which, taken from the tradition of monasteries, was designed so that each college building would always be inward-looking, a spiritual metaphor from the days when Christianity and religious training were the very focus of college life.

In the last 20 years, the University has been making an effort to redress the balance of men and women, and, with the last all-male college disappearing 16 years ago, the number of female students has been ever-growing. Equally, the balance of public school and state school students is improving; prejudice is in decline and, only 12 months ago, the first student from Scunthorpe was admitted into the fold.

Most colleges are free to visit, but opening times vary wildly, some are open all day every day, others for just five minutes on Shrove Tuesday. A few even charge steep entrance fees, but, as long as you don't walk around in a Hawaiian shirt taking photographs, it's not too difficult to slip unnoticed into the grounds.

While visitors are usually allowed to wander freely around the quads, chapel, dining hall and gardens, everywhere else is strictly out of bounds. Despite this, and the prominent 'NO ENTRY' signs, every year I hear stories of tourists, in search of toilets, inadvertently bursting into a student's bedroom to find not the urinals, but a pasty-faced youth in his underpants hunched over a copy of Ovid.

Without much background information on the colleges though, once you've wandered round one or two they can all start to look conspicuously similar. With some consideration, therefore, we have decided to concentrate on ten of the most prominent ones in the city centre, with maps, points of interest and a few tantalising stories for getting the best out of your visit. The other 29 colleges, incidentally, all resemble Oriel, except St Anne's, which looks like Sainsbury's.

An A-Z of University
Traditions
&Terminology

Balls

Once the exams are over in June, the parties really begin and, all over the colleges, lavish balls are held, the biggest (which is known as the Commemorative Ball) being at Magdalen, Worcester or New College. Expect string ensembles, bouncy castles, free booze, fairground rides, gambling and, if a band are playing, chances are it'll be something terrible from the Eighties like Bucks Fizz. Ticket prices for these can be astronomical, so it's not surprising there are clubs, such as the Oxford Stunt factory, whose sole mission is to gatecrash as many balls as possible.

If you want to try gatecrashing one of these events yourself, pull on some overalls and stride purposefully into the college, carrying a bucket of water; it works about five times out of every ten (although if this book sells well it might prejudice your chances somewhat).

Beating the Bounds

If you happen to be shopping in Marks and Spencer's on Ascension Day you might be alarmed to see twenty or so people enter, proceed to beat a metal cross in the floor with willow sticks, and then leave. This spectacle, however bizarre it may seem now, would have been fairly common centuries ago. Parish authorities then had a civil duty to  look after their own people and, in order to assert where their parish boundaries were, they would walk along them one day each year and beat them with sticks. Typically, Oxford decided to uphold the tradition and so every Ascension Day in the morning the parishes of St Mary the Virgin (SMV) and St Michael of North gate (SMNG) go around the town giving the walls a good walloping. It seems that M&S built over one of the boundaries and remain obliged, once a year, to let the loonies in. Look out for the glass case half way down the store on the left bearing the original boundary stone.

Bulldogs

These guys are the last remnants of when Oxford University had its own Police Force to keep students in order. They can still be seen patrolling the High after examinations making sure the students don't go bonkers with the egg-throwing, but otherwise keep a low profile these days. The last student to be shot by a Bulldog for 'undisclosed misdemeanours' was Carl Vincent in 1968.

Bumping

As you wander around the colleges, you'll probably notice that the walls of the Quads contain such graffiti as 'Merton bumped Balliol', 'Christ Church bumped Magdalen' or even 'Jesus bumped St. Hilda' (though we suspect this last could just be slanderous gossip).

This graffiti refers to the rowing races known as Torpids and Eights. In these two inter-college races the boats are lined up equidistant from each other, tip to tail, in lines of ten. Then they set off down the river. If a boat in 9th position catches up with the one in front and bumps it, they will swap places, unless they happen to bump a team who *didn't* get bumped the year before last, unless it's Oriel. Or St John's. There are four races, except when there are six (usually during the Chinese Year of the Monkey) and if a team bump the team in front on all four occasions, can recite the entire lyrics to American Pie, and demonstrate a rudimentary knowledge of how a rainbow is formed, then they become Head of The River and win a Teasmaid.

Collections

This is the name given to the examinations all students sit at the beginning of every term, although, rather confusingly, the end of term report (where a student is congratulated by his/her tutor *or* told to pull his/her socks up) is also known as a collection.

Oronyatekka Dining Society

The origins of this society stem from the last century, when the Prince of Wales was invited to Canada to hunt with some of its indigenous tribes. As a consequence, one chief's son was invited to study at Teddy College, where he distressed the Principal no end by eloping with his daughter.

The story has a happy ending, though, as, years later, he returned, having inherited a fortune, and donated lots of money to his old college. Oronyatekka's portrait now hangs there and he is still honoured today by this dining society (though, many would argue, in a rather dubious fashion as the group meet once a year for dinner in Indian 'fancy dress' and talk 'Indian' all night (e.g. matchbox would be 'white-man-magic-box-make-fire', etc). Then, supposedly, they rampage through town, making whooping noises, and end up at DTM, sitting in a circle around a pretend fire and smooching to Paul McCartney's 'Pipes of Peace'.

Dining Societies

Most colleges have exclusive dining societies, which students may be invited to join if their pedigree is up to it. Particularly popular in the 30s, there was, however, often a debauched and sinister element to them. One Brasenose society with 12 members was notorious for laying 13 places for dinner, the spare one being, naturally, for the devil. Nowadays, however, it's all twits in tails and white ties trashing a restaurant, then giving the owner a cheque with lots of 0s at the end to cover the damage.

Essay

'A collection of other people's thoughts disguised to look like your own, in the judging of which originality is heavily penalised.'
From Graham Chapman's excellent book: 'A Liar's Autobiography'

Exams

Should you spot students wearing pink, white or red carnations in June, it means that they're in the middle of their exams. The white one signifies they have their first exam, pink for the middle and red for their last. Keep a watchful eye out for those students with red carnations; tradition decrees that, after their last exam, friends and stranger alike will be at liberty to pelt them with eggs and flour and to empty tins of baked beans over their heads as a means of congratulation The pelting takes places over several days, culminating near the examination hall in the High Street, although any student caught in this vicinity with so much as a champagne bottle is liable to find him/herself fined by the University.

Feuds

While there are many long-standing feuds between several colleges in Oxford, none seem more antagonistic towards each other than Balliol and Trinity. There are a host of legendary stories about the different pranks each has played on the other, such as the time several Balliol students managed to break into Trinity Chapel and play the Muslim call to prayer, leaving the poor college no choice but to call in the Archbishop of York to reconsecrate the building.

The feud still continues to this day, and the emergence of the Harry Lime society in Balliol seems to have secured its future, as their sole aim is to apply lime-coloured paint to any sacred cows of Trinity College. Many years ago they painted Trinity's boathouse lime green, while another time they killed the coy carp in Trinity's fountain after turning the water lime green with a dye. It wasn't the dye that killed the fish but the washing up liquid they thoughtfully added afterwards for that foamy effect.

The all time classic, though, is when a wily Balliol student put an advert in a national paper advertising Trinity for sale. For months afterwards, the college had to tell every rich Americans that phoned up that they weren't open to offers after all. The article is now framed in the King's Arms*.

Lingo

Talking to unversity students for the first time can be intimidating and even a little frightening, owing to the vast array of bizarre and alarming colloquialisms exclusive to each college. If, however, you can befriend or tame one of them for just a few days they might take you into their confidence and teach you to say something like – *'Cynthia was using her face on this awful mirkin at the ball yesterday and within 5 minutes was giving him a real good jeffing'.*

Jeffing – From the verb *'to Jeff'*, meaning to snog in a cinematic or nauseating way.
Mirkin – any student who isn't from Oriel but whose knuckles still drag along the ground when he walks.
Using her face – to become animated and charming

*Thanks to Alex Dejonquieres for emailing several of the stories mentioned above.

Lodgings and dinner

All undergraduates lodge in the college grounds in their first year, but most have to seek accommodation outside the college after this. Food is provided for all students in the college, and formal wear is often required for the second sitting, except at Wadham, where black rollnecks and flares are mandatory.

Matriculation and Graduation

A chance to see the students spruced up and manicured at the Sheldonian Theatre, Matriculation is the formal welcoming of every scholar into Oxford, while Graduation is the final farewell. But, as both take place in the same building and in a similar fashion, it can be hard to distinguish the two, save for the fact that students are only allowed to wear their mortar boards after Graduation, while all Matriculation students have to carry theirs.

MAS

Unlike every other university in the UK, where one must study hard for another year to achieve this qualification, in Oxford all a graduate needs to obtain one of these is a crisp ten-pound note. Allegedly.

Oxford Time

If you hear Christ Church bell ringing at 9.05pm when your watch says 9pm, that's because some students' clocks still run on Oxford time. Time was standardised in Oxford with the birth of the railways timetable, but Christ Church refused to change. Typical.

Punks

According to a law passed in the 1970s, every college must have at least one Punk or Goth to add to its credibility, even if they are just public school boys with an identity crisis.

Rustication

Any student proving to be enough of a nuisance might find him/ herself in this predicament, which means they will packed off home for the year as punishment for a terrible crime (the ultimate being to copy someone else's essay). Oscar Wilde fell victim after returning to Magdalen two weeks late into term following a holiday in Greece. Despite this he still got a first.

Sconcing

This is an old tradition, often practised at formal dinners and drinking societies, whereby if a student (or don for that matter) challenges another to drink a yard of ale (two and a half pints), they must accept the challenge. But it seems that Christ Church students can claim immunity to the challenge on the grounds of being 'housemen', i.e. belonging to the House of Christ. This of course hasn't helped dispel the myth put about by Pembroke students that Christ Church students are nothing more than a bunch of lily-livered shandy-drinkers.

Scouts

These are the cleaners who sort out the rooms in colleges for the students, and are usually women. In the past, the scout's unofficial role was also as the confidant to the student, and often a surrogate mother/son relationship would develop from this. In Edwardian times wealthy scholars would often leave the contents of their wardrobe to their scouts (who in those days would have been male). These links have loosened over time and all a student is likely to leave now is a copy of Razzle and a couple of odd socks. In Cambridge, scouts are known as 'Bedders', which suggests that the unofficial mother/son role may have extended towards an unhealthy Oedipus complex.

Single Sex Colleges

There are no more exclusively all-male colleges in Oxford, although St Hilda's, by Magdalen Bridge, is the last to remain exclusive to women and the young ladies there are known affectionately as Hildabeasts.

Students and Dons

A Don is anyone who takes tutorials or lectures in the colleges and a student is anyone to whom they give the tutorial, except in Christ Church where Dons, rather confusingly, are known as Students, and the students as Rimmers. Hence the phrase 'I can't come out tonight, I've got to do a spot of rimming with my room-mate.'

Visitor

A visitor to a college doesn't mean a tourist but rather confusingly means someone who is a patron of the college e.g. The Queen is a Visitor of Christ Church, and Fidel Castro is a Visitor of Wadham.

Zebra

There are no zebras in Oxford.

A Guide to Oxford Students

"SPOD"

Spods

Found peeping over huge piles of books in the libraries and lurking around the pool table in the JCR, Oxford spods are an intelligent but geekish bunch who will undoubtedly get the firsts they so earnestly work for.

Distinguishing features range from bum-fluff facial hair to BO problems, while the more fashion conscious might sport a pair of Wrangler jeans. Perhaps unsurprisingly they rarely seem to have partners.

Home
St John's/ Merton/ Christ Church/ Corpus Christi

Favourite Drug
Cider and real ale

The Lights Are On But Nobody's Home

Despite being another hard-working group, this lot distance themselves from the Spods, partly because they know how to have a good time, but mainly because they fail all their exams. Rarely making it past their first year, those that do often hide their shortcomings behind amateur dramatics, although, unfortunately, they make lousy actors as well.

Home
Spread thinly throughout most of the colleges

Favourite Drug
Alcopops

The Yawning Majority

Sport, pleasure seeking, and mediocrity are what this lot are about, spending most of their days rowing and having a '*a seriously good time*', but always working just enough to keep their tutors happy. In the final year they will, of course, knuckle down, get a 2/1 or 2/2 and go on to get a good job at Arthur Anderson. Buying into the Oxford myth, the YM will enthusiastically organise the college balls and other events, all the time sporting their college scarves with no sense of irony. Found down the tackiest of Oxford's nightclubs wearing regulation smart shirts, cardies, and trousers from Gap.

Home
Exeter/ Worcester/ Jesus/ St Catherine's/ Pembroke/ Teddy Hall and many more.

Favourite Drug
Beer, and lots of it

"THE BEAUTIFUL PEOPLE"

The Beautiful People

Having chosen their college purely for its social status and wealth, these public school oiks from Holland Park see Oxford as utterly beneath their social class and only bothered to venture up here because daddy said it would look good on the CV.

Oxford's social life is, of course, way too provincial for them and they wouldn't be seen dead in any of the clubs here, preferring either to hang out at Freud's, or, better still, in London. Dress code is usually the same as the Yawning Majority, except the jeans are Gucci. Often to be heard uttering 'ciao baby', or 'cool'.

Home

Magdalen/ Oriel/ St John's

Favourite Drug

Coke, the powdered variety

Hacks

Politically minded, pompous, obnoxious and universally hated by everyone, including each other. Regulation dress usually includes jeans, tucked-in shirt, and tweed jacket. Despite having their sights on being the future Prime Minister, deep down they just need to be loved.

Home

Found loitering around the Oxford Union and OUSU.

Favourite Drug

The sound of their own voice.

"HACK"

Nerds

Male-only sub-species mainly comprised of frustrated Physics under-graduates sporting fleeces, long hair and jester hats as some sort of pathetic act of rebellion. Very much the outdoor type, really they're just Spods in juggler's clothing, who desperately want to be crazy, but the only way they know how is to go canoeing at the weekend.

Home

St Anne's, St Catherine's/ Wadham/ Balliol

Favourite Drug

Vimto/ Hi-energy drinks

"NERDS"

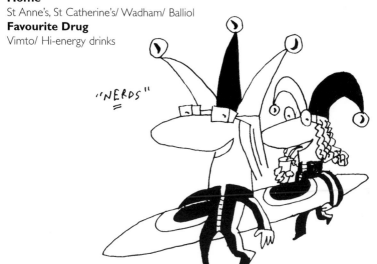

Slackers

Deodorant-shy public school boys with long hair and combat trousers. Slackers spend most of their time sitting in all day, smoking dope and listening to Nick Drake records, rarely venturing out, except to visit their allotments. Common among Law and PPE students, they will happily blow their entire grant on a new stereo, or a kilo of hash and spend the remainder of term eating nothing but porridge.

Home

Jesus/ Keble/ Pembroke/ Magdalen

Drug

Home-grown (and ketamine for the true professional).

"SLACKER"

"THE BLAZER BRIGADE"

Brookes Students

Up on a hill, far, far away, lies the university formally known as Oxford Poly, complete with its own unique range of outrageous stereotypes. At one end of the scale are the 'Blazer Brigade'. These are, of course, all those preppy boys and girls who planned on going to Merton, until they found that their A-level in Woodwork was not enough, so chose Brooke's as a way of legitimately claiming to have studied at Oxford, whilst praying that no-one ever snaps back with: *'Oh, which college?'*

At the other end of the spectrum are the Cowleyites, a collective of dope-smoking, counter-culture layabouts, who spend most of their time in the pubs on Cowley Road, or St. Clements, discussing Hunter S. Thompson novels, and only venture into the city centre to buy specialist Rizlas.

Brookes and University students rarely meet and both groups view each other with extreme distaste.

Home
Brooke's University and the Cowley Road
Drugs
Yes please

NB. Any student who doesn't fit these categories is merely a figment of your imagination.

All Souls College

All Souls College

High Street (01865) 279379
Open 2pm-4pm Mon-Fri Admission free

Set up in the 15th Century as a place of prayer and learning for the clergy, this college takes its name from 'all souls of the faithfully departed, a remembrance of the dead from the Hundred Years War with France in the 14th and 15th Century. Nowadays it is an eerily quiet graduate college for the elite. You don't apply to get in here, you get elected, although the most outstanding undergraduates can come and sit some gruelling exams to try and gain entrance.

There isn't a great deal to see at All Souls compared to many other colleges, but owing to its enigmatic character, curiosity might get the better of you. The college's most famous architectural features are the twin gothic towers in the Great Quad (overlooking Catte Street), and the large sundial, built by Christopher Wren, which sits on the wall of the Codrington library. All Soul's chapel is said to have been a regular haunt of Yeats who, despite having never studied here, used to enjoy hanging out here and composing poems on magic...

> Midnight has come and the great Christ Church bell
> And many a lesser bell sound through the room;
> And it is all Soul's night
> And two long glasses brimmed with muscatel
> Bubble upon the table. A ghost may come;
> For it is a ghost's right
> His element is so fine
> Being sharpened by his death
> To drink from the wine-breath
> While our gross palates drink from the whole wine.

From All Soul's Night by W.B. Yeats

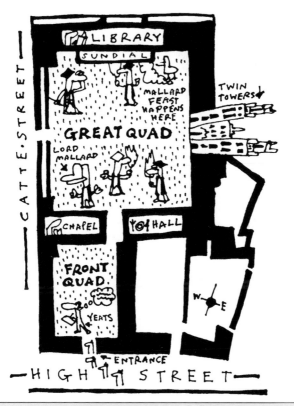

Oxford's strangest tradition: The Mallard Feast

At the beginning of every new century, tradition decrees that, after dinner on All Souls Day, Fellows and Masters grab sticks and torches and go wandering around the college grounds and rooftops pretending to search for the ghost of a mallard duck. Lord Mallard, who carries a long stick and wears a plastic beak around his mouth, heads the search and then, after giving up the ghost, everybody celebrates and sings the Mallard Song (the lyrics of which seem to be a closely guarded college secret).

This daft custom seems to stem from the fact that when the college foundations were being laid, a mallard was found in one of the ditches. It still begs the questions *'why?'* and, also, *'why don't they all go looking for earthworms, millipedes and moles as well?'*, but who's to argue with such a wonderfully ludicrous tradition?

The last Mallard Feast actually took place on January 14th 2001, and, though a large crowd turned up, including one crazy German couple who came over especially, little could be seen, expect for the odd glimpse of a semi-naked but heavily bearded man running across the rooftops squawking loudly (though this later just turned out to be Mick Taylor, the warden secretary, enjoying his night off). *The next Mallard Feast is due 2101. Can't wait.*

ALL SOULS

A game for one lonely player who has to use intellect, table manners and nepotism to get into this prestigious college. The rules of which are based on malicious rumours and idle gossip.

Round one

You have three hours to write as much as you can on a given subject. It could be anything from Politics to Beekeeping, depending how cruel they're feeling that day. This is followed by a translation paper from a language of the college's choosing. This, equally, could be anything from Esperanto to Welsh, so you'd better start brushing up.

Congratulations you made it!!

You are now a fellow of All Souls College and, as such, may stay here for up to seven years with free meals, lodgings and a salary. And, don't worry, academic work here is not compulsory; you can sit around in your pants all day and watch Richard and Judy if you want. Welcome to heaven.

Round Two

Well done, they were obviously impressed with your Welsh accent and extensive knowledge of bees. You will now be invited to an interview with some of the members of the college. This can be anyone that's ever studied here, so be prepared for quite a large ensemble. First you will be asked to name the Kings and Queens of England in reverse order and then there'll be a rigorous grilling of your family background, whom you know, and how much power your father has in Westminster. Namedrop as many important people as you can, especially anyone involved in politics or the media, and, above all else, try to be related to Lawrence of Arabia.

Round three

Sterling work, you're nearly there! You will finally be invited to dine with the college members. More than any other time in your life, be totally on your guard. To discover your true pedigree and etiquette you will most likely be served boiled artichokes and spaghetti. All eyes will be on you at all times so avoid slurping sounds and, for god's sake, don't suck the spaghetti from the plate. Whilst dining your peers will deliberately try to trick you by passing the port the wrong way and giving you the wrong spoon with which to eat your soup. Remember – be vigilant at all times and under no circumstances get drunk and start telling mother-in-law jokes.

Brasenose College

Brasenose College

Radcliffe Square (01865) 277830
Open 10am-11.30am for guided tours.
2pm-4.30pm Mon-Sun for general public. Admission £1

This college derives its name from its unusual bronze knocker which is shaped like an animal's snout and hangs above the main door. History records that it hung there happily for 100 years until the civil disquiet of the 1300s, when it was removed and taken to Lincolnshire by disgruntled students and teachers, who finally realised that to get on with their studies they needed a bit of peace and quiet. The knocker remained at the new college in Stamford until 1890, when the building came up for sale. Desperate to reclaim its precious snout, Brasenose simply purchased the whole building. The original knocker now hangs above the high table in the dining hall.

Brasenose has an enviable position in Radcliffe Square, close to just about everything and in beautiful surroundings. Enter from the High Street and you are in New Quad, which branches out into Deer Quad, one of the smallest quads in Oxford and said to be haunted by a cheerful ghost.

There are two contrasting stories as to how Deer Quad first acquired its name. The first suggests the name is ironic, being a subtle dig at Magdalen College's 'pompous' deer park. The other tells of a Blenheim deer hunt that once ended up all the way in Oxford. The deer, by chance, sought refuge in Brasenose's Chapel, but that didn't stop the hounds rushing in and killing it.

One guidebook I know even claims that the flowerbeds in Deer Quad are home to the Brasenose tortoise, although having not been seen for the last 13 years, fears about his ill health are steadily growing. Honestly, the rubbish some guidebooks will tell you!

Brasenose's Dining Hall, overlooking the Old Quad, is also worth a visit, as it is quite majestic. Behind its high table hangs the portrait of Alexander Nowell, the former college principal who, allegedly, invented bottled beer. A keen angler, Nowell used to take beer in bottles on his trips and the fashion caught on. Look behind him on his portrait and you'll see all his fishy paraphernalia. Opposite him hangs Betty Morley, the first lady in England to own a watch. You can tell she was proud of the fact, the portrait shows her holding it in her hand.

Heroes and villains

William Golding (author of 'Lord of the Flies')
John Buchan (author of 'The 39 Steps')
Jeffery Archer (the notorious jailbird only came here to do a PGCE and, although not officially attached to the college in any way, didn't bother to correct anyone who presumed that he had officially studied here)
Michael Palin (intrepid explorer, ex-Python and all-round good egg)

Look out also for the statues of the unicorn and lion taken from Brasenose's coat of arms. The unicorn was, for many years, stripped of its manhood (or should that be unicornhood?) until about 20 years ago when the offending member was replaced for anatomical correctness. This of course prompts the question – Where does one 'store' a unicorn's penis?

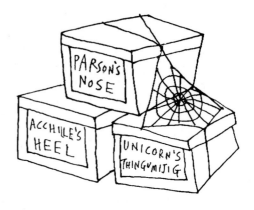

Brasenose is sometimes portrayed as being a breeding ground for rugger-buggers and Neanderthal sporty types, but this seems a little harsh, as, academically, it has produced some of the finest P.E. teachers this country has ever seen.

The Hellfire Club

In the 1820s this notorious club briefly flourished at the college. Not exactly Dead Poets Society, these guys were more interested in vice, drinking, black magic, and general miscreance. One of the more chilling stories about their antics begins in Brasenose Lane, for it was here that the then Vice-Principal of the college, Reverend Churton, while taking a midnight stroll, noticed a tall man wrapped in a black cloak, who seemed to be helping one of the ring-leaders of the club out of his window. The Vice-Principal ran forward, pleased at last to have caught one of them, but, as he sped towards the scene, an icy thought shot through him and he stopped frozen in his tracks. The student's window (like all others on the street) was tightly barred and access in or out was impossible. As Churton approached, in the gloom he could make out the agonised and twisted face of the student as his body was being pulled through the impossibly narrow gap between the iron bars.

When the tall man in the black cloak turned to face him, Churton saw what he described as 'The face of pure malevolence and horror'. He turned on his heels and fled back to the college, all the way to the unfortunate student's room, to find him lying on the floor, dead, and surrounded by the other members of the group.

The Hellfire club later confessed to having been halfway through a black magic incantation when the student started shaking and then dropped dead. Although none of the group would ever divulge the nature or reason for the invocation, they did agree to disband the Hellfire Club and that was the last Oxford heard of them...

Christ Church

Christ Church (also known as 'The House')

St Aldate's (01865) 276140 Open 10.30am-1pm & 2pm-4.30pm Mon-Sun
Admission £2 gallery admission £2

The largest and most visited of all Oxford's colleges, Christ Church is rich, has a diverse student population and, over the years, has produced a wealth of prominent politicians, writers and thinkers. It's not surprising, then, that together with its fame and imposing appearance, dozy tourists sometimes mistake it as the *only* college in Oxford.

In the middle of the college lies the magnificent Tom Quad; the largest quadrangle in Oxford. In the centre, the god Mercury does his best Bruce Forsyth impression, surrounded by the rooms and quarters of many important historical figures (as well as the odd loony).

Wander over to the far right-hand corner of the Quad and, under the stairs of the Great Hall, you should discover a door with the graffiti *'No Peel'* burned into it. This dates back to the mid-17th Century, when the Black Death was stalking the land and the college doctor (in the latter stages of syphilis and as mad as a brush) prescribed raw potato peelings as preventative medicine for the plague. The poor Christ Church students were forced to eat whole plates of the stuff with their breakfast and evening meals to stave off the dreaded disease. The graffiti appeared after a month of protests from the students and this revolting diet was quietly dropped, when the good Doctor was found wandering around Peckwater Quad *'hurling lemons and other citrus fruit at the students, and showing his genitalia to anyone who approached him.'*

Ascend the stairs to the Grand Dining Hall and you'll find it littered with paintings of prominent Christ Church men and a few kings and queens. There's also a portrait of Charles Dodgson (Lewis Carroll) on your immediate right as you enter, together with a stained-glass window, featuring characters from Carroll's books, just above the fireplace. Dinner is served twice in the evening; once at 6.30pm and again at 7.20pm, when only formal wear is allowed. To enter the hall for second dinner, according to college rules, jacket and tie must be worn at all times. Because of the ambiguity, however, of what to wear 'downstairs', shorts, underpants and even ladies' knickers have all been donned at various times by cheeky students.

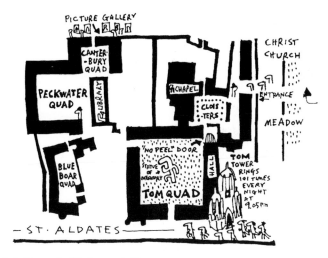

Christ Church Picture Gallery

At the Merton Street entrance to Christ Church, by Canterbury Quad, is a small basement gallery, with a modest collection for anyone passionate about Renaissance Art or sketches from old masters. If you're visiting with children, get them to look out for the gory Strozzi painting of Judith from the Old Testament story, holding the severed head of Holofernes. A hastily improvised story comparing Holofernes to Harry Potter should keep the kids interested for a good 15 seconds.

Christ Church Chapel

I have heard that a way to avoid Christ Church's steep admission fee is to claim you are going to the chapel to pray. Although I haven't tried it, there does seem to be a ring of truth in this, as the chapel is the official Cathedral for the diocese of Oxfordshire, so if you dress smart, look pious and fake the local accent, you should get in for free.

One strange tale I heard about the chapel dated back to the 1980s, when someone hit upon a unique way of raising much-needed funds for repairs to the roof by installing a jukebox that played *'holy hits'*, from 'Jerusalem' to 'Spirit in the Sky', for 50p a go. But complaints arose when a copy of *'Too Drunk to Fuck'* by the Dead Kennedys was sneaked in by some wily students and the embarrassed Dean had the jukebox removed.

Tom Tower

Up on the top left of Christ Church, overlooking the Head of the River pub is this famous tower, built by Sir Christopher Wren. Hanging here is the seven-ton mass of Great Tom, a bell which still chimes 101 times at 5 past nine every night. This was the old curfew bell, rung once for the 101 students of Christ Church to remind them to be back in college grounds. Nowadays it is used by the students as a reminder that Happy Hour in The Bear is just about to end.

William Buckland

One of Christ Church's most notorious eccentrics was William Buckland, who, in the 1900s, was first professor of Geology here and lodged in one corner of Tom Quad.

WILLIAM BUCKLAND EATS HEART OF LOUIS XIV

Buckland, not content with keeping a bizarre menagerie of livestock in his room (which included a jackal and a bear) and sharing his dinner table with his horses, was also quite singular in his eating habits. His dinner guests would often be bemused and a little horrified when presented with mice fried in batter, stewed badger and even worm fritters. In fact, as his eccentricity grew, Buckland rather fancied attempting to eat every living thing. Legend has it that, whilst dining with the owners of Nuneham Park one evening, he was proudly shown a shrivelled piece of flesh, and asked to guess what it was. Before he could be stopped, Buckland had gobbled it up. His hosts were mortified; he had just swallowed their most treasured heirloom – the heart of King Louis 14th.

The Jabberwocky tree

Heroes and Villains

John Locke (Philosopher)
Charles Dodgson (a.k.a. author Lewis Carroll)
W.H. Auden (Poet)

Harry Potter

Visitors to Christ Church these days will be hard pushed to miss the Harry Potter connection. Having had their dining hall staircase used for several scenes of the second Harry Potter film, and the hall itself used as template for the one in Hogwarts, the college has found new fame amongst the ankle-biter population; visit in summer and you'll find them swarming around the place, waving their wands, and trying to turn all the custodians into newts.

If you're also a Harry Potter fan and want to find the staircase, it's in the far right-hand corner of Tom Quad. Stand at the bottom of the staircase with your back to the 'No Peel' door, and the view through the alcove is actually the shot in the film where Harry and the gang return from the lake. (A lake and a wall were actually built here just for this shot.)

Corpus Christi

Corpus Christi

Merton Street (01865) 276700 Open 1.30pm-4.30pm Mon-Sun Admission free

With a reputation for liberalism and friendliness, Corpus Christi, though small and sandwiched between Merton and Christ Church, should not be overlooked; it is still one of most beautiful colleges in Oxford. Richard Fox is said to have founded the college in 1517, but went blind before it was built. Legend has it that on its completion, Fox was lead around the front quad twenty three times to avoid any crushing disappointment at its size.

Corpus Christi's best-loved feature is the sundial in the centre of Front Quad, by which operates not only by the sun but also the moon (although, being set to Oxford time, it's always five minutes slow). At the top of the sundial sits a majestic golden pelican, which was part of the coat of arms of its founder and is the most common symbol associated with the college. In fact, animals seem to crop up a lot in Corpus Christi's history. In the Middle Ages a fox, three owls and several bees were kept chained up as college mascots and, for many years now, Corpus Christi has been involved in the rather bizarre annual tortoise race between Balliol and Brasenose. There is even an official role of 'Custodian of the Tortoise' in the JCR. Corpus Christi's current tortoise is Hermione, although she doesn't actually belong to the college but is loaned by one of the professors. It was only a few years ago, however, that she was at the centre of a small scandal when it was discovered that someone had given her a line of speed before the race to make her go faster. Despite this Hermione didn't win, but just stood around shaking and grinding her gums for a few hours.

There are 117 gargoyles around Corpus Christi, so you probably won't spot them all but do look out for the carving of the bird feeding its young in the corner of College Tower. Pass through Front Quad and the tiny cloisters until you reach the garden at the back and you will be rewarded with a splendid view of Fellows Garden, Christ Church Gardens and the meadows. Finally look out for David the gardener; if he's not too busy and likes the look of you, he'll probably share a few good tales about the place.

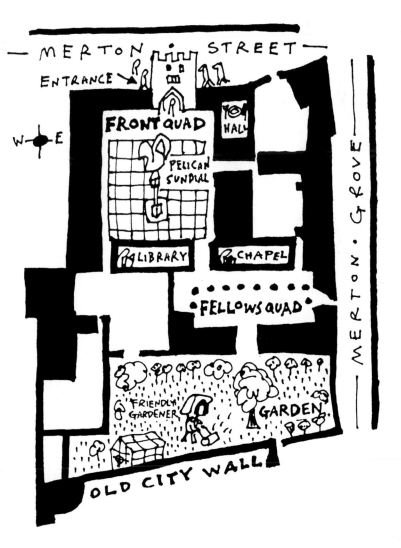

Magdalen College

Magdalen College

High Street (01865) 276000 Open 1pm-dusk every day (with some variations in summer)
Admission free

Magdalen is simply one of Oxford's most glorious colleges, boasting its own deer park, a riverside walk and some beautiful architecture. Pronounce the name *Mag-da-len*, however, and you'll immediately blow your cover; the correct pronunciation is 'maudlin' (or if you're American, '*mawwwdlin*'). One of the college's main architectural attractions are The Cloisters, which, once you're through the front entrance, are reached through the archway to your right. This beautiful enclosed quad is host to many strange gargoyles and statues which were, at one time, brightly painted and are said to have

inspired C.S. Lewis's stone statues in Narnia. You should be able to spot deer, camel, dragons, griffins, wrestlers and jesters, together with Moses, Jacob, Goliath and several human heads.

Behind St Swithun's Quad is Magdalen's famous Deer Park. The forty or so deer arrived in 1708 and, with the exception of a few tortoises and the Wadham Penguin, they are the only animals now kept within University grounds.

On the far right of the college grounds, a wrought iron gate leads to a riverside path which is extremely peaceful. A watchful eye might spot a kingfisher along the river here. Look also for the gate and bridge which lead to an island in the Cherwell. In the middle lies a water meadow also used for the deer, and, if you're lucky enough to be around in March or April, the whole meadow appears to be cloaked by a purple mist when the fritillaries are in bloom. With all this in mind, it's not surprising that Magdalen is sometimes the subject of envious mockery by some of the poorer colleges, who can only afford a small tarmac quad for their students. In fact, there is a famous story of one rival college, who, in the late 1890s, got so fed up with everyone marvelling at the deer, that it decided to outdo Magdalen once and for all by building a Giraffe Park. It must indeed have been stunning sight to see these magnificent creatures wandering amongst the buildings and quads, but, alas, within only four weeks every single one of them had been captured or killed by rustlers from nearby villages and for a brief period in Oxfordshire, giraffe rugs and coats were rigueur.

Oscar Wilde

Wilde is one of Oxford's most infamous undergraduates. He studied at Magdalen from 1874 to 1878, where he indulged his love of aestheticism and fresh-faced young men with pert behinds. A brilliant scholar, Oscar was so confident of his success that he is famously said to have read about his First in the Times whilst breakfasting in The Mitre one morning.

One of the lesser-known stories about Wilde tells of how, one day, four students, singularly unimpressed with Wilde's foppish behaviour, decided to ransack his room. Upon discovering these miscreants, Wilde, being a big fellow at well over six foot, single-handedly ejected them all and frogmarched the ringleader to his own room, rolled him up in a carpet and piled furniture on top of him. He then calmly opened up the felon's most expensive bottle of wine and invited any onlookers to join him in a glass.

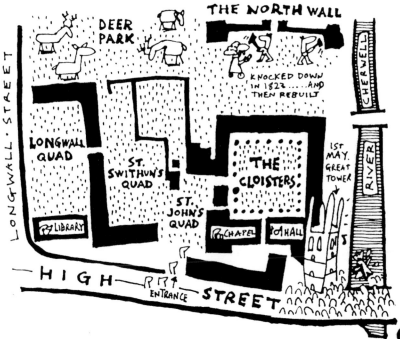

The President, the Wall, his Wife, her Moustache

At the back of the college grounds sits a rather idiosyncratic building known as the North Wall. This marks the beginning of a Georgian classical quad, which was to be built here in the late 1700s to replace the Cloisters (which were getting a bit tatty). The North Wall was just the first part of this new wing, but the money ran out and there it stood.

Now it just so happened that, during the 1800s, Magdalen had a rather eccentric president; Martin Routh. Routh took power in 1791 and held onto it until his death in 1854. Though he kept his marbles until the end, Routh despised change, and continued wearing knee breeches and a wig all through the 19th Century when the fashion had moved on somewhat. He was also known for wearing a long cassock under which his concealed feet would take tiny delicate steps, giving the impression that he was on wheels.

Because of Routh's ardent resistance to change, it came as something of a shock to the college when, on a whim one early morning in 1823, he called in the builders and had the North Wall completely demolished. This rash act very quickly caused a national outcry and to Routh's great reluctance the North Wall was painstakingly rebuilt, *stone by stone*.

Routh got more disagreeable as the years dragged by, although he did succumb to Cupid's Arrow in his mid-sixties when he married a lady of a certain age whose moustache was said to be legendary. In later years, Routh's health declined, his steps got shorter and shorter and, finally, he ended up being carried from his lodgings to chapel in a Sedan Chair, the spectacle of which became quite a tourist attraction.

When Routh died, Charles Daubeny, a Magdalen scientist who had always despised Routh's policies, took one of the president's wigs to a special spring at Matlock in Derbyshire which, owing to its special mineral content, was known to petrify any object dropped in it. Routh's wig, once immersed in, became hard as stone and still hangs to this day in the old library.

Heroes and villains

Dudley Moore (pint-sized comedian, Jazz pianist and one-time partner of Peter Cook)
C.S. Lewis (author of the Narnia books)
John Betjeman (poet)
William Hague (failed politician who single-handedly made baseball caps deeply unfashionable)

Merton College

Merton College

Merton Street (01865) 276310 Open Mon-Fri 2pm-4pm weekends 10am-4pm
Free admission £2 Guided tour of Library, Max Beerbohm Room and Chapel (Enquire at lodge or phone for details of the tour)

Located down the quiet cobbled antiquity of Merton Street away from the bustle and pollution of the High, this college, founded in 1264, probably lays the best claim to being Oxford's oldest college.

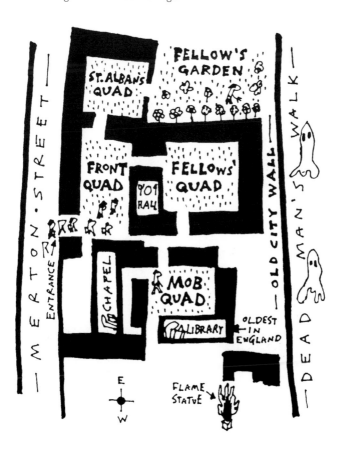

On the far right inside Merton lies Mob Quad, the oldest in Oxford and the blueprint for most of the other quads in Oxford and Cambridge. At the back of the college stands part of the old city wall, and a 'flame' statue. The latter was erected to honour Sandy Irvine, a student who, together with Mallory, perished near the summit of Mount Everest in 1924. (To this day no-one knows if they were actually on their way up or down.)

One of the best ways to experience Merton is to visit on one of the summer evenings when the college mounts a series of concerts in its chapel. On occasions like these, hidden away from the modern part of the city it's easy to imagine that you've been transported back 100 years to the era of Beerbohm and T.S. Eliot. Eliot didn't romanticise the town though. Oxford wasn't much to his liking, as he explained –

'As an American I have always enjoyed the company of women but in Oxford there seem to be none.'

Merton's Ghosts

As one of the oldest colleges in Oxford it would be surprising for Merton to escape the odd ghost story and in fact it boasts two.

One spectre, who haunts the upper library, is believed to be the ghost of Duns Scotus, a medieval philosopher and passionate academic who just couldn't bear to leave behind the world of Oxford, and so vowed to remain in the library for ever. Many claim to have seen his upper torso wandering through the library at midnight, meaning his lower half is presumably dangling in the room below, yet none have as yet validated this particular theory of mine.

The other ghost is that of Colonel Francis Windebank, who was court-martialled in 1645 for having supported the king during the Civil War. He is believed to have been shot at the city wall, which now makes up the back wall of Merton College overlooking Christ Church Meadow.

Windebank's ghost is said still to wander along Dead Man's Walk late at night and some claim that if the cows ever moo on the stroke of midnight, then the Colonel is walking abroad. Either that or the kebab van men are on the prowl again.

The tour of the Old Library and Max Beerbohm's Room

The Old Library, complete with all its musty smells, slowly decomposing tomes and ancient foundations, was set up in the 14th century and is one of the oldest surviving of its age. Many of the original books are in Latin and the one still chained to the bookcase is a reminder of how precious they once were, or, at least, how light-fingered the students were. (The 'great unchaining' of the books took place in the late 18th century, when all the students swore on Scout's Honour not to steal them.)

Thomas Bodley's chest, with its ornate and elaborate locking system, is worth seeing too, though, as the whole library is incredibly gloomy, it makes me wonder how anybody saw anything at all in the days before electricity (candles were banned for obvious reasons) and, as beautiful as the small, original stained-glass windows are, they utterly fail to relieve the place of its darkness. And finally, anyone turning up for the tour in 'unsuitable footwear', be warned. Show up in high heels or spiked running shoes and you will be forced to wear a pair of giant-sized slippers known as 'Green Shufflers' to preserve the ancient tiled floor. And, believe me, you will feel a right Charlie sliding around in them.

From the library the tour moves to a room dedicated to one of Merton's most celebrated students – Max Beerbohm (or, the 'Incomparable Max'). Max, who studied here in the 1890s, was a good friend of Oscar Wilde's, unsurprising really as he too was a great wit, a dandy and a celebrated author in his own right. Beerbohm's best-loved work is his only novel 'Zuleika Dobson'; a playful and fantastical tale set around the fictional 'Judas College' (based on Corpus Christi next door?) in which he manages to lampoon the stuffiness of Oxford's academia, the sheep-like nature of its students, and the silliness of its traditions, all in one comic serving.

The room is furnished with some of Beerbohm's belongings from his villa in Italy and decorated, appropriately for his time, in primrose yellow. On display you'll also find his Top Hat, cane, savagely brilliant caricatures, and a self-portrait (which reveals Max to have had more than a passing resemblance to the late, great James Stewart).

Heroes and villains

Max Beerbohm (author of Zuleika Dobson)
JRR Tolkien (author of The Hobbit, Lord of the Rings and indirectly responsible for Marillion)
TS Eliot (author of The Wasteland)

New College

New College

Holywell Street and New College Lane (01865) 279555
Open every day in summer 11am-5pm via New College Lane Admission £2
Open 2pm-4pm October-Easter via Holywell Street Admission free

Despite both of its entrances being slightly off the beaten track, New College is worth seeking out as it is one of the more unusual colleges Oxford has to offer, and, at first glance, appears to have been built on the ruins of a castle. In actual fact, the college was built around a fair stretch of the old city walls, which explains why parts of the college still have embrasures.

At the far end of the grounds, Garden Quad has an intriguing feature in the centre; a large mound (once the burial ground at the time of the Black Death) which, if you are a student here or are bold enough, you can scale to sit at the top and be king of the castle. A friend, Ellie, who studied here, told me if you stand in front of the mound and clap your hands, it squeals. I was a little dubious at first, but, after a couple of times, discovered it to be true; it sounds like it's having a tiny orgasm.

In New College chapel, the disturbing and contorted figure of Lazarus is said to have given Nikita Kruschev a sleepless night during his visit here in1958. In contrast, the whole of the chapel wall at the far end is filled with carved figures like the lost army of China, which are, in fact, a multitude of saints, patriarchal figures and angels.

Trivia-wise, a brief scene from the Bond film 'Tomorrow Never Dies' was filmed here. You know how in every Bond movie, he gets caught 'on the job' somewhere near the beginning of the film and *always* at the end? And usually in a boat?

In *this* film he's at New College canoodling with some Danish student when his bleeper goes off and M gives the usual '*where the devil are you Bond?*', to which he replies - '*I'm just brushing up on my Danish.*'

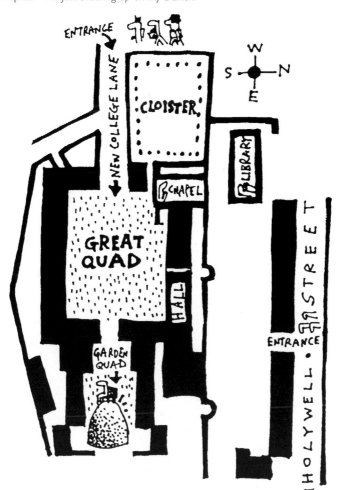

Heroes and villains

Viriginia Woolf (author of 'To the Lighthouse')
John Fowles (author of The
Collector and The Magus*)
Tony Benn (groovy politician and
self-confessed tea-addict,
consuming over 40 cups a day!)
Dennis Potter (television
playwright whose work included
The Singing Detective and Cold
Lazarus)
Reverend Spooner

(the old warden of New College who was responsible for inventing
Spoonerisms. This is where you get the first syllable of two words the wrong
way round and has led to a whole host of 'hilarious' comedy names such as
Kenny Everett's 'Cupid Stunt' and Russ Abbott's 'Friar Tuck')

*I once met someone who came to Oxford to do English literature and in her first
term studied The Magus as an example of a failed novel. I read it two years ago
and, apart from the pretentious Greek quote at the end, thought it was wonderful.
Obviously, I need to do the degree to find out where I went wrong.

Oriel College

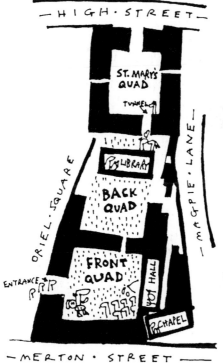

—HIGH·STREET—

ST. MARY'S QUAD

TUNNEL

LIBRARY

BACK QUAD

ORIEL·SQUARE

MAGPIE·LANE

FRONT QUAD

HALL

ENTRANCE

CHAPEL

—MERTON·STREET—

Oriel College

Oriel Square (01865) 276555 Open 2pm-5pm Mon-Sun Admission free

For many centuries this college's official name was – 'The house of the blessed Mary in the Oxford commonly called Oriel of the foundation of King Edward the Second of famous memory sometime King of England.' Then, one day, someone suggested just calling it 'Oriel', and there was an enormous sigh of relief.

Originally a training ground for prominent priests, in the 19th Century Oriel became a powerhouse of intellectuals, but since the war, its reputation has been principally for rowing, drama and music. One of its most celebrated students was intrepid explorer Sir Walter Raleigh, who brought back a pound of potatoes and Twenty Marlboros from his travels, which proved popular with the masses. As with Merton College, the best way to experience Oriel is to come and see one of the Shakespeare productions they stage every year in the Front Quad.

A Scandal at Oriel

The tunnel that leads from Middle Quad to Back Quad was once the scene of a minor scandal during the First World War. The girls from Somerville College had been housed in the Back Quad while their college was taken over by the medical services during the First World War and, to stop the men in Oriel getting too 'acquainted' with the girls, the tunnel was bricked up. Mysteriously, however, one night a 'hole' appeared and, legend has it, a few cherries were popped that night. Not taking any more chances, the Provost of Oriel and the Principle of Somerville went down to guard the tunnel and remained there day and night for the rest of the war, in order to uphold the dignity of the two colleges (and to avoid any lawsuits).

Dastardly deeds

For many years Oriel was proud of its unbroken record as Head of the River, but in the winter of 1991, the Secretary of the University Boat Club allegedly erected a notice in secret at Exeter College forbidding all rowing practice on the river owing to the danger of ice. Oriel, of course, never saw the message and so set out the next morning for their usual practice. After 15 minutes they too decided it was too dangerous to row but that was enough time for them to get nobbled by the boat club for breaking the rules.

At the hearing, the secretary is reported to have clapped his hands in glee and said *"let's dick Oriel"*. They were penalised for boating illegally and were dropped four places from Head of the River where they have remained now for over 1000 years.

A cheeky tale

Many years ago I visited Oriel to see a production of Hamlet. It had been raining heavily for two days and we, the audience, were seated on a raised platform underneath a canopy of overlapping sheets of transparent tarpaulin. It wasn't raining that afternoon but, there was a cold wind whipping around us as we huddled together watching the play.

Hamlet, alone on the stage, was contemplating life and death in his famous soliloquy when, unexpectedly, the wind whipped up one of the sheets of tarpaulin from above our heads, suddenly freeing about 10 gallons of rainwater that had been trapped there. In a short but torrential downpour, it managed to completely drench one poor sod who was sat underneath.
If that wasn't enough entertainment, watching Hamlet giggle his way through 'to be or not to be' made it indeed a moment of rare comedy I shall never forget. Thank you Oriel and Aeolus, God of Wind.

Ladies, a warning!

Not the most progressive of colleges, Oriel was the last to admit female undergraduates into its folds and today, in the college bar, women are still only served half pints in ladies glasses and are required to wear ankle-length skirts at all times.

St John's College

St John's College

St Giles (01865) 277300 Open 1pm-dusk every day Free entry to quads and garden

The college grounds of St John's hold quite a few surprises for the visitor. Enter via the front and it leads you straight onto the college's famous Canterbury Quad; a fine example of Baroque architecture. Some would say that the portals within the logias have enriched entablatures and I'd be inclined to agree with them. More importantly, if you've got kids, the lions and unicorns lazing in the niches of the arches are fun to look out for.

St John's most celebrated features, however, are its gardens, perhaps the finest of all the colleges and extending all the way from St Giles to Parks Road. With their long lawns, exotic flowerbeds, and regal trees, if the sight of a clump of Dizzy Lizzies gives you a secret thrill, then these gardens will not disappoint. If you happen to venture left through the college you'll no doubt stumble across a cocoon of modern buildings serving as student accommodation. One part is the Beehive, so-called for its two-storey polygon feature. Beyond that is a micro-nation of featureless, grey, concrete angular buildings linked with a sort of sunken garden theme, except without the garden, and all serving as a reminder that Prince Charles still has a point about modern architecture.

As well as having a reputation for academic excellence, St Johns has its own literary greats, and in the 1950s a writers group called 'The Movement' was led by fellow students Philip Larkin, John Wain and Kingsley Amis. In recent years Amis has fallen somewhat out of fashion for his misogynist and rightwing views, and of the three Wain seems best-loved in the town, having written a passionate trilogy charting the struggles of a modern Oxford family. Tony Blair is another famous alumni, and, by all accounts had a reputation as something a ladies' man. When he wasn't wooing the girls, he was practicing with his rock band 'Ugly Rumour' and prancing about in Cuban heels, medallion and open shirt.

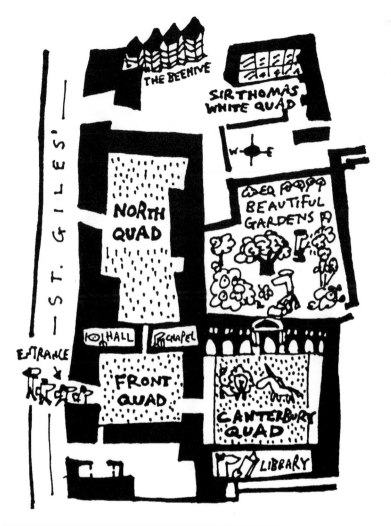

Heroes and villains

Kinglsey Amis (author of Lucky Jim and father of Martin)

Philip Larkin (poet)

Tony Blair (ex-rock musician turned Prime Minister, turned dictator)

Robert Graves (writer)

John Wain (the writer not the actor)

Jethro Tull (the agricultural reformer not the hairy folk/rock combo)

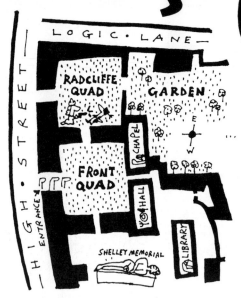

University College

University College

High Street (01865) 276602 Not open to the public

University is another one of those colleges hanging on to the tedious claim of being the oldest in Oxford. In fact University was once *so* keen to hold this title that, in the 14th Century a forged document appeared declaring University College to have been set up by King Alfred in the 900s. This was taken as gospel until the 19th Century when, at a coming out party, after a lot of nervous coughing and red faces, the college admitted that the documents were forged and eerrr, it wasn't really err *that* old and err…. Twiglet anybody?

The college's two best features are its chapel, with its unusual 17th Century stained glass windows depicting stories from the Old Testament, and the Shelley memorial. There is nothing quite like this in the whole of Oxford and, for this reason, it's a shame that University is permanently closed to visitors. Fear not, if you write to the domestic bursar and ask for permission to view it, he should let you in. Failing that, I leave it to your own devious minds as to how to arrange a viewing.

The Shelley Memorial

The English Romantic poet, Percy Shelley (1792-1822 A.D.), was at University for less than a year before he decided to circulate a pamphlet entitled `The Necessity of Atheism', which caused a bit of a stink. Although Shelley never admitted to writing it, the University got rid of him anyway for *'contumaciously refusing to answer questions about the authorship.'*

In 1891 however, his daughter-in-law had a statue of him built for the British Cemetery in Rome, which proved too big to fit in the post, so she offered it to University College along with a large wad of cash. University suddenly decided that perhaps Shelley wasn't all that bad after all, and had the statue set in a separate little room inside the University.

The room features a marble slab with the naked and dead Shelley lying upon it, while, underneath, a bronze statue of the muse of poetry looks up lamenting. Over the years this room has been a gift to undergraduate japes, and while Shelley's tummy banana has been painted a whole host of exotic colours, the muse has also been known to sport a multitude of comedy hats and, on one occasion, the Times crossword was even found open on its lap. Nowadays the statue is sealed off from any potential pranksters, but can still be viewed in all its Victorian gaudiness. To find it quickly, go in the main entrance (adopt a lofty air of superiority if you're not a member of the university), take a sharp right through staircase 3, keep going along the corridor et voila!

Necrophilia and University College

Eminent physician Thomas Southwell rented rooms here in 1420 and became well respected for founding the College of Physicians in 1441. On a less respectable note, however, he was caught committing necrophilia with the late Duchess of Gloucester and was thrown in the tower of London, where he died the night before his execution. Since then, necrophilia has fallen out of fashion in University College and hardly any students are put to death for it these days.

The Great Shootings of 1892

In 1892, a master with a reputation for giving the most tedious lectures in the whole of Oxford had a daughter who was engaged to a Fellow of the college. All seemed fine, until this Fellow's murky past was revealed in the guise of a wronged woman, who turned up at the master's lodge looking for him. She was shooed away but soon returned with a gun, hell-bent on revenge. She had it in mind to shoot the first person she saw, which, unluckily for the master, happened to be him, although the wounding did not prove fatal. The wronged woman was arrested and imprisoned, but disgrace on the Fellow led to the end of the engagement and he resigned from the college.

After the whole thing had calmed down, the students did at least hope that the master's lectures were going to be a bit more interesting, but all the shooting had done was to give him a pronounced stutter, which made them worse than ever.

Heroes and villains

Stephen Hawkin (responsible for making black holes fashionable)
Armando Iannucci (comedy writer for Steve Coogan)
Richard Ingrams (founding editor of Private Eye)
Bill Clinton (dope-smoking sex maniac and former president of the world)

Shopping

At first sight Oxford doesn't appear to offer much in the way of shopping unless novelty lava lamps, university sweatshirts and inflatable chairs are on your must-have list, but with a few markers from our exhaustive shopping expeditions, over the following pages the more intrepid bargain-hunter might discover a few intriguing places in which to find hidden treasure.

Around Carfax in the city centre, the shops are a typical blend of high street chains and tourist traps, but once off the beaten track, your labours will be more rewarded. Little Clarendon Street is a good starting point, with its wild array of ethnic artefacts, retro gear and objects for the home, while, just off George Street, Gloucester Green is home to some pretty cool record and clothes shops and a market every Thursday.

Surprisingly, there are few antique shops in Oxford, considering the number of tourists (especially American) who want to take home something 'authentically English' but have to settle for a packet of digestive biscuits and a football. In contrast, however, there are a plethora of second-hand bookshops, whose prices, as a rule of thumb, increase in proportion to their level of dust.

No shopping experience in Oxford, however, would be truly complete without a trip up the Cowley Road. With its health food shops and last decade's New Age fashion boutiques, promising 'honestly cheap goods', it could be dismissed purely as a hippie Mecca. But, in fact, the shops here sell everything from musical instruments, skateboards and vintage clothes to teapots and saris, so don't be surprised after an afternoon here to find yourself whizzing home on a new set of roller-blades, wearing a fetching tie-dye suit, and clutching a sitar.

BORDERS OXFORD

9 MAGDALEN STREET OXFORD OX1 3AD
TEL: 01865 203901

OPENING HOURS:
MON-SAT 9AM-11PM/SUN 11AM-5PM

ALL EVENTS ARE LISTED ON OUR WEBSITE
WWW.BORDERS.CO.UK

2ND TUESDAY OF EVERY MONTH:
ODEON FILM QUIZ

LAST TUESDAY OF EVERY MONTH:
BORDERS MUSIC QUIZ

ISN'T IT TIME YOU READ A BOOK?

BORDERS BOOKS, MUSIC AND CAFÉ HAS OVER 120,00 BOOK TITLES,
25,000 CD'S AND OVER 5,000 DVD'S AND VIDEOS IN STOCK AS
WELL AS AN EXTENSIVE RANGE OF MAGAZINES AND NEWSPAPERS

BOOKSHOPS
BIG GUYS

Borders
9 Magdalen Street (01865) 203901

This American chain stocks by far and away the city's best range of magazines and spoken word tapes, as well as the odd book. And to complete their Yankee status they've even got a Starbucks at the back of the ground floor, where the impoverished student (or merely tight-fisted) can borrow a copy of 'the Economist/ Viz/ Tractor Weekly/ Skin Two' from their shelves, pore over it, get it covered it in coffee and jam and slip it back on the shelves without spending a penny.

Blackwell's
Broad Street (01865) 792792

This is Oxford's oldest bookshop, and certainly the most cherished amongst the college fraternity. In fact the greedy beggars have, not one, but four bookshops on Broad Street. While their music and art shops are self-explanatory, Blackwell's Too (near to Waterstone's) specialises mainly in children's books, and the Oxford Bookshop sells all things connected with the city, from local literary giants to the book in your hand.

If you happen to be browsing in the main store (next to the White Horse) and haven't been before,

don't miss having a look at the Norrington room in the basement, and prepare yourself for a shock. You know how in every Bond film there's a scene where the villain is in his office stroking a cat and he nonchalantly presses a button to reveal a futuristic labyrinth with thousands of workers doing dastardly deeds just behind the bookcase? Well it's sort of like that down here too; it feels like the very nerve-centre of the town. If the computers went down in here….who knows? Maybe all the students would grow mullets, the shark would melt, and Oxford United would score a goal.

Waterstones
Broad Street (01865) 790212

Nestling on the corner of Broad Street and Cornmarket, Waterstones have the sort of location that other shops would happily sell their metaphorical (and literal) grandmothers for. I'm glad to say they exploited their good fortune wisely, with friendly, well-informed staff and four floors of books on every subject you can think of.

THE LITTLE GUYS

*'Nobody ever saw anybody actually
open a second-hand bookshop'*
Albanian proverb

Comic Showcase

19/20 St Clements
(01865) 723680
Open 10am-6pm Mon-Sat

Excellent range of comics, with TinTin,
Asterix and Calvin and Hobbes for
the young at heart, to the more
serious collectors' stuff from the likes
of Kevin Smith, Chester Brown and
Alan Moore. Then there's Marvel back
issues; X –Men, Spiderman, Star Wars...

The Inner Bookshop

111 Magdalen Road (01865) 245301
www.innerbookshop.com

Once tucked away behind a butcher's
on the Cowley Road, this shop has
now houses one of the best
collections of esoteric and occult
literature in the UK. Books on spiritual
sciences, gurus, holistic medicines and
mythology vie for shelf space with
David Icke paperbacks and re-issues
of the Fabulous Furry Freak Brothers.
The stock is incredibly comprehensive
and there's a handsome collection of
affordable second-hand stuff too.

As with the notice board in the
Magic Café next door, this also is a
good place to learn more about the
New Age, Martial Arts and spiritual
type courses on offer in Oxford.

For those who believe there's more
to life than reality TV, lifestyle
magazines and indoor bowling, I really
can't recommend this shop enough.
And it's all thanks to the hard work of
its long-term owner Anthony (he's the
one who looks like he used to roadie
for the Grateful Dead).

Jericho Books

48 Walton Street
(01865) 511992
www.JerichoBooks.com
Best to phone for specific opening times, as
the awkward buggers seem to have different
times for almost every day of the week
(though you can't go wrong between
twelve and five).

When so many of the second-hand
bookshops in Oxford seem to stock
nothing but first editions of Jane
Austen and obscure 18th Century
farming manuals, it's good to find a
place that makes room for cult and
esoteric stuff. Along with the usual
academic and humanities sections,
they've got a meaty selection of mind-
body-spirit stuff, and sci-fi for those
who know their Vonnegut from their
Von Daniken.

Curiously, the owner, Frank, was
recently murdered in a rather grizzly
fashion but it hasn't dampened his
spirits much, as it was in a crime novel,
(though he doesn't know which one).
If any of you bookworms out there
know the book do let him know; the
suspense is killing him.

Oxfam Bookshop

56 St Giles (01865) 310145
Open Mon-Sat 10am-5.30pm

Oxfam's first exclusive bookshop has a fair selection of books on virtually every topic and is constantly supplied by a growing host of donors (Radio 3 presenter Humphrey Carpenter and the late Iris Murdoch have both given generously in the past).

Watch out for the stairs at the back, however; many is the time I've been perusing the History Section and nearly tumbled backwards down them into Social Sciences. Remember – good research can saves lives.

RECORD SHOPS

Massive Records

95 Gloucester Green (01865) 250476
Open 9.30am-6pm daily, 12-5pm Sunday

By far the biggest collection of modern Hip-Hop, Jungle, Techno, Garage, House, and other Electronica, in Oxford. And all on vinyl too. This is also a good place to check out club nights and other events from the fliers or by chatting to the staff if you can stop them dancing, that is.

Avid Records

4 Gloucester Street
(Just off George Street) (01865) 200411
Open 9.30am-7pm Mon-Sat
11am-4.30pm Sun
www.avidrecords-uk.com

In case you didn't already know it, vinyl is back, big time. Throw away all your nasty CDs and return to a world where big is beautiful and analogue is god. And where better to start than Avid, as they have a superb collection of quality used records. Don't expect any great bargains here; these guys really know their stuff (and their prices), but do expect to find a plethora of quality records and exceptional gems, particularly if you're into Jazz, Soundtrack or Underground Pop. Last time I was here, I joyfully parted company with £20 for an ultra-rare Woody Allen album in mint condition. As well as all the Rock, Pop, and Jazz on the ground floor, upstairs is a wealth of Classical, Folk, Comedy, 45s and Soundtrack, while Dance, Techno, Breakbeat, Hip-hop, Drum and Bass, old George Formby 78s and a very friendly man called Gary are all skulking in the basement.

A word of warning! Because of the sheer amount of stock, the aisles are incredibly narrow, and you'll find yourself having really to squeeze past people as you desperately aim for the Jazz section in the far corner. Come on a Saturday with a pram and a fat friend and you'll create a four-day gridlock.

The Record Fair (at the Town Hall)

Monthly Admission £1 (or thereabouts)

If you're looking for modern stuff like Electronica, American Lo-Fi, Post-rock or strange Break-Beat, forget it; the weirdest thing you'll find here is an old Stereolab LP. If you're just on the lookout for some Sixties vinyl or CDs at knockdown prices you'll probably be happy. There's a good selection of Rock and Pop, especially Indie from the 80s and 90s. There's even a modest selection of Jazz and Soul. If you don't find anything worth buying though you still might feel a little bit cheated after paying a pound admission.

Polar Bear

183 Cowley Road (01865) 251443
Open Mon-Sat 10-6pm, Sun 11am-5pm

This independent record shop, half way up the Cowley Road, is a godsend for anyone with a passion for the latest underground sounds, and their recommended section on the wall speaks volumes as to the kind of cool music they're into (Beck, Sigur Ros, White Stripes, Boards of Canada etc). They also have a good selection of local music from such labels as Truck and Shifty Disco, while obliging staff will fill you in on the best local bands and gigs.

DNA

1-3 St Michaels Street (01865) 790568

Colourful and trendy street fashion for the girls (they don't stock stuff for the guys any more). Look out for the world's largest pair of jeans hanging on the wall.

SS20

131 Cowley Road (01865) 791851
www.ss20.com

Cool little skateboarding shop selling hats, videos, clothes and other skate gear. It's not cheap, but then you can hardly go out skateboarding in M&S cardies can you? They also do board hire.

Oxford Boot Store

Located in the Covered Market

Worth a visit just to see the shop's two mechanical cowboys. JC stands in the window, driving the staff to distraction with his monotonously tapping stick, while Gabby, a full-sized cowboy, sits in a chair by the till, singing and telling stories to the customers. And if you yell 'Yee Haaw' from the other side of the shop he tells the funniest joke I've ever heard.

Cult Clothing

Unit 7, Gloucester Green (01865) 794454

Probably the biggest fashionable clothes shop in Oxford and certainly the most established, with tons of big label names and a heavy slant towards club-wear and street fashion. If you can't afford their prices but still want something 'hip', then the sale shop up the road in Friar's Entry sells their cut-price stuff. Trivia buffs may be interested to know that Thom Yorke once worked here, and some say that, on cold winter's evenings at the stroke of midnight, his whining can still be heard, emanating from just by the cut-price shirts.

CLOTHES SHOPS

Queen's Street is your first port of call if you're just looking for the chain stores. Topshop, Next, New Look to Burton, French Connection, Gap… all the usual suspects are here. For your slightly more up-market ladies shops, you'll find Oasis and Karen Millen in St Ebbes; Jigsaw, Coast, and Whistles all at the top of the High Street, near Carfax Tower and FCUK, Gap and Monsoon on Queen's Street. For men, I'm afraid the story's not so good. The conservative clothes shops (of which there are many) will want to dress you up like Stephen Fry or Prince Harry, while the painfully hip ones just cater for that ubiquitous Eminem-style, urban, street look. True, there are a few good second-hand shops but, if you're a natty dresser and looking for more, it's a trip to London I'm afraid.

SHOPPING

Bicester Village

(just off Junction 9 of M40 and
about ½ hour drive from Oxford)

This is one of those sprawling
outdoor shopping complexes with
dozens and dozens of big-name
clothes chains and discount shops
selling brand names at half price.
Some people find these places
ghastly but, if you're into all the
chains and designer labels, the
choice here is far superior to what
Oxford has to offer and often
much cheaper.

SECOND-HAND CLOTHES

Bead Games

40 Cowley Rd (01865) 251620
Mon-Sun 10-6pm

Taking its name from the Hermann
Hesse novel, this is something of an
Aladdin's cave that has always
reminded me of the clothes shop in
Mr Ben. Try on one of their fake
leopard-skin coats and you might
mysteriously find yourself on a
jungle adventure.

Beyond doubt, this has to be the
most interesting and flamboyant
collection of second-hand and new
clothes anywhere in Oxford. Expect
to find everything from corsets,
basques, French lingerie, Kameez,
PVC and fake fur to jewelled
trousers, hand-knitted jumpers, snow
boots and traditional peasants'
jackets. Keep your eyes peeled for
the Marlboro jacket too!
Its rather eccentric owner, Erica, also
makes clothes out of old velvet
curtains and saris as well as doing a
neat line in bizarre and silly
postcards, French brollies and wands.

More recently she's been running a
'1001 Bohemian Nights' hire service
meaning you can get kitted out in
Sergeant Pepper attire, or have a night
on the tiles with your partner as
showgirl and pimp (your choice as to
who wears what).
*We also have the best collection of
facial hair in Oxford'* proclaimed Erica,
last time I was in, prompting me to
wonder who (if anyone) had the
second-best.
Oh, and she also sells beads.

Uncle Sams

25 Little Clarendon Street
Open 10am-5.30pm Mon-Sat

This retro clothing paradise on Little
Clarendon Street has been run by its
friendly owner, Bob, for nearly twenty
years (I even remember when they
used to have a parrot in the window)
and is still a real gem.

Spacious, colourful and clean, Uncle
Sam's has an excellent range of quality
vintage 60s/ 70s gear including fake
furs, leather jackets, duffle coats,
sheepskins, old Levis, kooky sunglasses,
shirts and denim-wear. Whether you
want to look like an extra from the
Sweeney, Happy Days or Performance,
you'll find it here.

108

Unicorn

Ship Street, Opening times a mystery

One of the strangest second-hand clothes shop I've ever visited. With its owner seemingly unable to throw anything anyway, the shop is now *so* full of clothing that actually getting in is becoming a struggle, never mind trying to have a look at anything. Mix that with the gloomy lighting and you have a recipe for disaster.

Every time I visit, the owner is trying to have a clear out but, 14 years down the line, if anything, it's getting worse. But I offer these minor quibbles out of affection, and look forward to the day the back room is liberated once again so I can have a proper nose around the suits and jackets.

Vintage Clothes

Cowley Road
Open 10am-6pm Mon-Sat
(01865) 251345

Run by three brothers – Alex, Jonathan and Edward – the stock here ranges from top hats, Safari helmets and pin-stripe velvet suits (a bargain at £75 each), to copies of the Chap. They also promise more Saville Row suits for the future.

COOL THINGS FOR THE HOME

Little Clarendon Street

*Not only a bohemian denizen of coffee-houses and restaurants, but Little Clarendon Street, or Elsie (LC) as it's known, also doubles as **the** place to buy stylish furniture, chic household items and other natty things for the home.*

Ottoman specialise in nick nacks and the kind of coffee table/ novelty books you'll pick up and flick through, but never buy.
Up from there is **Sylvester's**, yet another one of those novelty item shops, which stocks the usual array of funny shaped clocks and lava lamps (surely everyone's bought one by now??). And did they really once have a T-shirt in the window that had -
'*All this and my dad's loaded*' scrawled across the chest?
Who buys this stuff??

If Habitat is a notch up from Ikea, then **Central** and **Ligne Roset** are a notch above Habitat (see diagram). Central stock a cool but expensive range of stylish modern furniture, kitchenware, gadgets and object d'art, while French designers Ligne Roset lean more towards things for the office.

If ethnic stuff is more your bag there's **Tumi** at the top, where you can kit yourself out like the pan-pipe band from the Fast Show, or **Oriental Crafts** lower down, with a selection of Eastern paraphernalia and, notably, some rather lovely Chinese crockery and soup bowls.

Ladder of sophistication

CENTRAL
HABITAT
IKEA
EDINBURGH WOOL SHOP

Central 33-35 Little Clarendon Street (01865) 511700
Oriental Crafts (keep your nose peeled for the smell of incense)
Ottoman 31 Little Clarendon Street (01865) 311393
(Open Mon-Sat 9.30am-6pm Sun 11.30am-5.30pm)
Sylvester (you can't miss it, unfortunately)
Tumi (listen out for the panpipe music)

Antiques on High

85 High Street (01865) 251075
Open Mon-Sat 10am-5pm, Sun 11am -5pm
Discounts available on cash purchases

Having moved from the old Jam factory, these guys obviously have an attachment to breakfast condiments as their new premises used to be the offices for an old marmalade factory. Inside is surprisingly large, housing over 30 different stalls and cabinets, displaying watches, jewellery, books, old sheet music, ceramics and even Roman coins.

The prize for the oddest customer request still goes to the man who came in looking for a chain on which to hang the 3 bullets he'd recently had dug out of his chest.

The Fishbowl

118-122 Magdalen Road
(01865) 241825

It's a wonderful feeling coming here and losing oneself in the endless corridors of strange and beautiful fish; they've got everything – piranhas, tiny sharks, marine invertebrates, lobsters, coral and eels. They even used to stock octopi but the owner told me they kept climbing out of their tanks and scaring the children. A haven for fish-lovers or anyone wanting to treat their partner to an exotic dish dinner.

THE ANNUAL CHEEKY AQUATIC CREATURE AWARD (SPONSORED BY TRILL)

Most expensive fish
Red Arowanna, at £3,600

Dullest-looking fish
Red Arowanna

Ugliest fish
Pseudopimelodus Fowler/ South American Catfish (it resembles a fat, ugly Salvador Dali)

Silliest fish
Bubble Eyed fish (the Marty Feldman of fish)

Cutest fish
Striped damsels (looks like a Humbugs with fins)

St Clement's Antiques

93 St Clements (01865) 727010
Open 'all day, every day'

Run by the mildly eccentric Giles
Power, and specialising in the more
'bizarre and unusual' antiques, this is a
collection of curiosities, ranging from
clockwork spits to Giles himself. On
entering, visitors instantly relinquish all
rights to leave empty-handed unless
they agree to partake in a number of
fruitless games, all made up by Giles
himself to while away the hours.

The ⊛LDeST CUri⊛SiTY in the Sh⊛P

Examine every item in the shop carefully. Employing what scant knowledge you
have of antiques, try and guess the oldest thing in the shop (apart from Giles).
Guess correctly and you instantly win a 20% discount off any item in the shop.

Loosely based on some old TV show, in
this game you are challenged to identify
the object pictured on the right. Supply
Mr Power with the correct answer and
win a whopping 20% discount off anything
in the shop.

Wood you believe it?

Bring into the shop *any* wooden item (from a totem pole to false leg) and Giles will
attempt to guess what kind of wood it's made of. If he fails I suspect you may be
entitled to some sort of discount.

VinMagCo

High Street (01865) 240859

Open 10am-6pm Mon-Sat, 11am-5pm Sun

A Valhalla for movie buffs, music lovers and fans of the glamour of yesteryear, this shop stocks photos of your favourite actors, movie posters, models, toys, books, T-shirts, and Elvis Monopoly boards (what next?). They've even got a framed copy of Michael Caine's birth certificate on offer for forty-odd quid.

It's interesting to note that, while anodyne and vacuous girl/boy bands rule the airwaves, the most popular idols (according to the guy working here) are still Audrey Hepburn and Sean Connery. Step aside Geri Halliwell and Liam Gallagher – there's hope for us yet.

MARKETS

The Covered Market

High Street and Cornmarket

Set up countless years ago to relieve the congestion of traders on the main road, the covered market is a wonderfully odd jumble of old-style cafes, bookshops, heelers, butchers, florists and fish stalls, juxtaposed with modern clothing outlets and shoe and gift shops. It's well worth spending some time idling your way through the aisles here; there are some curious outlets to see, and no Oxford experience would be complete without a cup of tea and a snack upstairs at Georgina's. And lovers of good food owe it to themselves to seek out the very excellent Oxford Cheese Company and Feller's Organic Butchers. In fact, vegetarianism aside, to see the market at its best come at Christmas, when the butchers hang up their poultry, wild boar and other festive meats and the whole market takes on a somewhat Pickwickian feel.

Gloucester Green Market

Every Thursday 8am - 4pm

Arts, crafts, collectables and antiques can all be found here. Delve further into the rows of stalls and you'll discover a world of hippy clothes, picture frames, boots, old prints, rugs and throws, candles, light shades, crockery and second hand books.

COSTUME RENTAL & AND PARTY SHOPS

Party Mania

179 Kingston Road (01865) 513397
Open Mon-Sat 9.30am-5.45pm

If you keep following Walton Street deep into Jericho you'll eventually stumble on this place. The shop has a good selection of costumes for hire and every novelty joke item you can think of, from remote-controlled fart machines to penis pasta.

Dominated by the larger-than-life personalities of Jenny, Jessica and Jane, (the latter two being Jericho's answer to Mrs Slocombe from 'Are You Being Served', and Margo from 'The Good Life'), they spend the day sharing their saucy humour and bizarre anecdotes with the customers.

Apart from the predictable mass of blokes buying fake breasts for their mates 'Stag Do', their customers also include many of Oxford's white witches, who usually hire medieval garb for ceremonies.

The city's resident werewolf also used to pop in at one time to buy rubber chickens (?) and other essential werewolf items. Mary said –

"He's got the typical one eyebrow, hairy face and sunken forehead. When he first came in, he tried to convince us that he was a werewolf, and we didn't believe him. But since his stories about the things he got up to in the caves in Wooton-Under-Edge, he really has got us all wondering…"

And in case you're wondering, in the photo Jenny **is** holding a wedding bouquet penis!

Celebrations

Market Street (01865) 202608
Open 9am - 5.30pm Mon-Sat

Run by the cheerfully rude duo of Barbara and Pat, Celebrations stock a good selection of fancy dress, party stuff, jokes and other novelty items. In summer, students flock here in their multitudes for the tradition of giving balloons and flowers as post exam gifts. Stuck for a gift for a loved one? They also sell 'Shit in a Can.'

The Ballroom

5/ 6 The Plain
(01865) 202303/ 241054

When the near-legendary Sweet Charity outgrew its home on Cowley Road, the owner simply lifted up her cocktail dress and ran around the corner to bigger premises. Run by a handful of charming ladies, this is *the* place to go if you're off to a ball or fancy something different for a night down DTM. Stocking the usual array of DJs and other formal wear for men and over 3,000 dresses for the ladies, it doesn't, however, stop there. For the more adventurous, there are Lord Byron-style frilly shirts, Spats and gangster suits, Austin powers costumes and several gimp outfits. Prices for hire are reasonable and, upstairs, you'll find a modest selection of used suits, velvet jackets and cocktail dresses for the less solvent. Be warned however, should you get embroiled in a food fight and lose, expect a hefty cleaning bill.

Catering for your wildest culinary appetites and more besides, Oxford has some excellent curry-houses, a diverse selection of Mediterranean and modern continental restaurants, and, for the less adventurous, over 30,000 pubs in the city-centre, all serving traditional microwave lasagna. Try some of the cafes and restaurants on the High Street for a touch of sophistication, the likes of Le Petit Blanc, or Al Shami in Jericho, for some really outstanding cuisine, or the Indian and Jamaican restaurants on the Cowley Road at the weekends for a full-on party atmosphere and great food.

There really is a wonderfully rich choice of places to eat on offer in Oxford, but, despite all this, McDonalds still seems the most popular destination for visitors. If only the likes of the Grand Cafe and Gee's gave away free plastic Star Wars figures with their yak's cheese salad and crème brulee, I'm sure things would be a lot different...

The vast majority of restaurants/ cafes reviewed below have been chosen either because we like them, they have been recommended to us, or they happen to be run by members of our family. For the penny-conscious, we have included prices of typical meals for each.

   All restaurants reviewed have veggie options.

CAFES

CITY CENTRE & JERICHO

Georgina's

Avenue 3 Indoor Market High Street
(01865) 249527
Open Mon-Sat 8am-5pm
Baguettes £4-5

Upstairs, away from the crowds, fishy smells and carcasses of dead flesh that litter the covered market, this small, ramshackle café has been second-home to countless university students for as long as I care to remember. From its bright colours, bamboo blinds, and movie posters stuck on the low ceilings, to an ever-changing array of attractive young staff in their orange flowery T-shirts, Georgina's has always had an easy-going, chic and shabby charm that contrasts sharply with the ever-growing glut of stylish, but austere, cafes in the city centre. The food here is typical for the student crowd it's catering for; they do a good range of snacks such as paninis, nachos, bagels, omelettes and baguettes and, like all good cafes, breakfast is served all day.

The perfect spot for idling away an afternoon with friends, or, alternatively, just come on your own, stuff your face and curl up in a corner with a copy of OK! to read about the latest bit of Michael Jackson's face to have fallen off.

afternoon cream teas. For drinks you can choose from fresh coffee, tea, cocktails, beer, wine and soft drinks.

This café even claims to be on the site of the first coffee house in England (1650) and, to celebrate its antiquity, has daubed Milton quotes on the wall which are the only things that somehow spoil the decadent charm of the place. Well worth a visit, even if just to slurp your way through a Baileys latte or to sample their delicious chocolates. The cappuccino cake comes highly recommended.

The Grand Café

84 High Street (01865) 204463
Open 9am-6.30pm. Available for hire.
Main Course – Rare Roast Beef Plate £9.50

A cross between Buckingham Palace and Rick's bar in Casablanca, The Grand Café is a definite contender for Oxford's classiest joint. The food fits the surroundings in terms of price and style and, as well as salads and sandwiches for lunch, they do

The Jericho Café

112 Walton Street (01865) 310840
Mon-Thurs 8am-10.30pm,
Fri & Sat 8am-11.00pm, Sun 9am-6pm
Breakfast around £6

This welcoming North Oxford café has been around now for over ten years, and is as popular as ever for its salads, Mediterranean food, sandwiches and daily specials. It also makes a good breakfast café, as the laid-back atmosphere is conducive for lounging around of a morning and reading the morning papers (as plenty do).

Georgina's

The downstairs area is perfect for those seeking a little peace and quiet, while the notice board on the stairs is useful for catching up with local goings on. Find out who to call to get your cat exorcised or where to do a spot Brazilian dancing. And, if you get bored of the music, they'll even let you put on your own CD.

The News Café

1 Ship Street (01865) 242317
Open 9am-9pm Typical meal £6-8

Rather like Georgina's in the covered market, this has been a popular student haunt for many years, although its big advantage over its competitors is that it stays open really late. Meals range from about £4-£8, with the usual offerings of bagels, paninis and various hot dishes and specials of the day. With a smoking area upstairs, plenty of mags and papers scattered around the place (from Private Eye to the Dandy) it has a pleasant, convivial and unhurried atmosphere. If they only served breakfast all day and got rid of the telly, it'd be perfect.

St. Giles Café

St Giles (01865) 552110
Open Mon-Thurs 8am-3pm, Fri-Sat 8am-5pm, Sun 8am-4pm Greasy fry-up £3.50

Smoky and cramped, with surly staff cooking up heart-attack inducing fry ups, St Giles café is, of course, nothing short of a bloody marvel. In fact this timewarp greasy spooner has been the saviour of malnourished and impoverished students since the late 1700s and shows no signs of decline. This is a veritable arcadia for meat-lovers and anyone who likes their food every colour of the rainbow except green. All the classics are available here – steak and kidney pie and chips to beans; sausage, bacon and omelette – with portions to satisfy even the greediest Americans, and all at terrifically low prices. During its busiest hours expect the grumpy staff to get grumpier, and don't be surprised to be turfed out your seat seconds after finishing your meal to make way for the next wave of hungry carnivores. Nothing short of an institution.

COWLEY ROAD CAFES

Baba

240 Cowley Road (01865) 203011
Open 5pm-10pm, Mon-Fri for food
(but until 11pm to drink),
11am-11pm Sat-Sun Hunters Mezze £9.90,
Green Mezze (veg) £8.50

Great Moroccan-themed snack menu from which you can choose either combos or singletons. Wash down with a nice bottled lager, move onto the cocktails and – hey presto – you've had a most pleasant evening out!

Café Coco

Cowley Road
(01865) 200232
Open everyday 10am-11pm.
Breakfast 10am-12pm.
Tuna £8.95 Pizza £5-8

This Mediterranean-style café at the bottom of Cowley Road has a French-colonial flavour to its design and food, and is a popular haunt for the Cowley Road residents and student population.

While the choice here is a bit limited (the menu mainly consists of pizzas, fish and salad), the food is of good quality, plus they're not stingy with their portions. Merguez is a North African dish with lots of tasty ingredients and comes recommended for the meat eater. Remember also to keep any eye out for the specials board.

If you fancy just dropping by for a drink, you can sit in the middle of their Cheers-type bar and get so drunk that you'll imagine you can see a clown having a bath in the corner.

Top tip: During the evening, Café Coco gets very busy, so if you don't like smoke-filled rooms beware; it seems that all Cowley Road descends here some nights just to have a fag.

EXCELSIOR CAFÉ

The Excelsior Café

Cowley Road (01865) 248504
Stuff floating in grease £4

Come, enter the strange and frightening world of the Excelsior Café, a cross between Twin Peaks and a Mike Leigh film. The dense cloud of cigarette smoke and the permanent sound of hacking coughs lend the café a unique ambience that is utterly beguiling. And, while the manager glides slowly around the room taking orders in his deadpan Boris Karloff voice, the other customers in the café sit motionless, staring vacantly into space.

Although the menu includes such delights as Horlicks, spaghetti and chips, and jelly and ice cream, I'd only really recommend it for that hangover-cure greasy spoon breakfast. And don't try asking for anything fancy. Last time I was in I asked for the breakfast without beans and my girlfriend wanted her eggs sunny side down and no tomatoes. The waiter stared at us, wrote nothing down, and served us two standard breakfasts.

If you like an element of surrealism and horror with your eating experiences, this is the real McCoy. And be sure to ask for their Arabic Cannon and Ball mug for your coffee.

Joe's English/American Café Bar

21 Cowley Road (01865) 201120
Open 10am-11pm daily, 10am-10.30pm Sun
Joes Burger £7.25, Chicken Salad £8.50,
Roast Med veggies £8.50

Formerly Joey's, this friendly, slightly chic, café is particularly popular for its hearty transatlantic cuisine of burgers and cooked breakfasts. You will walk out of Joe's very full so make sure a taxi is waiting to whisk you straight home – you won't be able to walk. This being Oxford, they also do cocktails, with which you can wash down your hamburger and fries. Occasionally, live acoustic musak may accompany your meal.

CHINESE

The Oriental Condor_

20 Park End Street (01865) 250988
Open 12pm-11.30pm.
www.oriental-condor.co.uk
Average dish prices - meat £5.20, prawn
£6.00, vegetarian £4.40

Authentic and sparse in style, with an extensive menu including plenty of veggie and meat dishes. It's common to see Chinese people eating here – always a sign of quality. Beware, however, the awful karaoke-style music!

The Rice Box

178 Cowley Road (01865) 202138
Open Mon-Thurs 12pm-2pm 5pm-midnight, Fri-Sun 12-3pm & 5pm-midnight
Thai Chilli Chicken £4.60, Bean Curd
Mixed Veg £4.10

Situated half-way up the Cowley Road, this place is perfect if you're in a hurry or if it's late and you want a quick but healthy bite, as the food here is tasty and usually takes no more than 5 minutes to arrive. It's always heaving Fridays and Saturdays so don't expect a table, but during the week is generally fine.

NB. This is not a place for a night out, but a fast-food joint for the more discerning.

FISH

Fishers Restaurant

36/37 St Clement's Street, near Magdalen
Bridge (01865) 243003
Open Lunch Wed-Sat 12pm-2.30pm, Sun
12.30pm-3pm. Dinner Sun-Fri, 6pm-10.30,
Sat 6pm-11pm. Salmon fishcakes £9.25,
Seared Tuna Steak £13.95

Fantastic fish restaurant championed by several friends who rate it as their favourite Oxford eatery. The fish is delivered fresh from Cornwall and Billingsgate (big fishy market in London) most days, so you know you're getting good quality ingredients. With this in mind, try lobster from Nova Scotia, Salmon Fishcakes (my girlfriend's favourite) or good old-fashioned fish and chips, although, at nine quid, this is not Harry Ramsden's. They're low on veggie options, but compensate elaborate blow-outs for 'fish enthusiasts' e.g. Fishers Hot Shellfish Platter comes with mussels, crevettes, scallops, cockles, prawns and langoustines!

Add to this pleasant service and a nice, chatty atmosphere and you have a recipe for success. Sitting near the large windows may mean you get passers-by gazing at your seconds, but that's a small price to pay.

Top tip – if you've children, this is ideal as it's kid-friendly: they even supply crayons! They also offer varieties of lunchtime 'deals' that are worth keeping an eye out for.

Loch Fyne

55 Walton Street (01865) 292510
Open Mon-Thurs 9am-10pm. Fri 9am-10.30pm, Sat 10am-11pm. Sun 10am-9.30pm
www.lochfyne.com
A fresh fish meal is typically around
£12 (plus veg)

Now we normally try to steer clear of restaurant chains, as there are plenty of independent restaurants to choose from without funding the economies of scale on which the chains thrive. However, scruples aside, Loch Fyne does really excellent seafood, and, besides, Scotland (particularly the west coast, where Loch Fyne is situated) is a bonnie place.

Top tip – try the seabass.

FRENCH

Café Noir

3 Osler Road, Headington (01865) 741300
Open Mon-Sat 9.30am-11pm,
Sun 12pm-10.30pm
Main meal typically £12 (pasta £8.50)
Crepes come with veggie options (£8.95)

Small, French restaurant-bar with a calm, romantic atmosphere.

The service is laid-back and friendly and in the summer months you can sit at the pavement tables for that authentic Parisian feel (though it is a bit close to the main road). The food here is of a high quality and I recommend the Monkfish.

Le Petit Blanc

71-72 Walton Street (01865) 510999
Open 12pm-3pm 6pm-11pm Mon to Fri,
Sat 12pm-3.30pm & 6.30-11pm,
Sun 12pm-3.30pm & 6.30pm-10.30pm

Owned by Raymond Blanc and Richard Branson, this is a popular restaurant in the heart of Jericho with chic, convivial surroundings and excellent food. The menu changes every two weeks, with a particularly fine selection of puddings and an extensive wine list. Keep your eye out for the good value set menus between 12pm and 3pm if you want to try this food on a budget.

Friendly and accommodating to everyone from ankle-biters to B-list celebrities. Watch out, however, for Richard Branson; he's notorious for scrounging taxi fares and never paying them back.

INDIAN & BANGLADESHI

The Aziz

228-230 Cowley Road (01865) 794945
www.aziz.uk.com Open 12pm-2.15pm,
6pm-11.30pm daily £6.50 Chicken Bhuna,
Chicken Patia £6.50, Dimmdamm (veg) £5.50

One of Oxford's best Indian Restaurants, as much for its décor and friendliness as its food. Their excellent curries and good service should guarantee your speedy return. And if you become a real regular, the manager might even start to tell all about the famous people that eat here. I once saw Jeremy Paxman collect a takeaway in his slippers (he was wearing his slippers, not using them as a vessel for the curry). It's a good idea to book, as it gets busy most nights.. Recommended

Chutneys

36 St Michaels Street (01865) 72424
Open 12pm-2pm & 6-10.30pm daily
Lemon Chicken £7.95

Centrally located, bright and modern inside, Chutney's offer fresh, tasty and stylishly presented dishes, though, on the two or three occasion's I've eaten here recently, none of my meals were piping hot. And it is a bit annoying that the staff here can, at times, be grumpy. Gripes aside, it is always incredibly busy here, and for a reason; the food really is a cut above most other curry houses in Oxford.

Mirch Masala

137-139 Cowley Road (01865) 728581
Open 6pm-11.45pm daily
£9.50 for 3-course buffet

The Mirch has had a few facelifts over the years, the most recent of which transformed it from run-down deli to a thriving Indian buffet. It's a spacious, cheery restaurant and the buffet system seems to work; order your drinks and nan, fetch your starter (salad, popadoms etc.), eat starter, relax, fetch your main course, eat main course, relax. There's a choice of twelve labelled dishes, including at least four veggie. It's a welcome change to have a taster of three or four dishes rather than the usual Chicken Bhuna. I am assured that all are prepared earlier the same day and there's no doubt they taste as fresh and tangy as they always have done, though sometimes the food can be a little tepid. The buffet system allows you to eat almost immediately and you can refill as many times as you want, which simply means you leave the restaurant clutching a swollen belly. Speaking of which, this is Oxford's most child friendly 'Indian'. The Mirch also has a number of large tables; ideal for birthday/party bookings. Takeaway menu available.

ITALIAN

La Capannina

247 Cowley Rd, (01865) 248200
Open 12pm-1.45pm (not Mondays),
6pm-10.30pm Mon-Sat, Sun 12pm-3pm
only Typical main course – pasta £4.90-
9.50, meat £8.90-£13.90

Our Oxford bred friend, Teresa, used to visit this restaurant when she was 8 years old (she's now about 33) and reliably informs me that the waiters, the menu, and the crockery are still the same! This is home-cooked Italian cuisine at it's finest and not your typical pizza and pasta joint. I can wholeheartedly recommend the Agnelotti (a veggie pasta dish) and the Beef Bracioletti Special (thin strips of beef rolled round a filling of pine nuts and sultanas!). They also do a Tiramisu to die for. The friendly and experienced staff will make you feel even more at home.

Top Tip – if you're having trouble finding La Cap, just keep your eye out for the log cabin opposite the Bingo hall on Cowley Road.

JAMAICAN

HiLo

68-70 Cowley Road (01865) 725 984
Open 7pm-12.30pm,
1pm-3pm for lunch at weekends
Spicy Chicken rice and veg £8ish

Far, far away in a universe all its own sits HiLo, a Jamaican restaurant and late-night drinking-den. Well, alright, it's actually on the Cowley Road, but you know what I mean.

Poles apart from the vast majority of Oxford's formal and conservative restaurants, HiLo seems to open and close when it feels like it, has no set menu and, so I'm told, customers are charged according to what the owner thinks they can afford.

Offering the usual standards of red snapper and Jerk chicken as main courses and sweet potato, breadfruit and plantain for starters, the service too, is typically Jamaican and can be very slow, so relax, take advantage of their range of bottled beers and you can't go far wrong.

The place itself is wonderfully ramshackle; it always looks like they're halfway through moving in, with boxes of yams lying around, paintings sitting on the floor and the rather alarming toilets that, at weekends, look like they've survived a hurricane. And the décor here is at odds with pretty much the rest of Oxford, for, while the back room is, for no good reason I can think of, full of old reel to reel machines, the walls here are adorned with everything from chalkboards, informing the casual observer of house rules (NO SWEARING, NO FEET ON FURNITURE, NO CAMERAS), to raunchy Jamaican calendars from the early Nineties. As for the ceiling – look out for their delightful scrotum sack lighting.

Open until roughly half twelve (give or take an hour), come here for an after-hours drink and, some nights, it'll feel like you've stumbled across the fantastic party that all your life you suspected was going on but no one had invited you to. Other nights again, for no apparent reason, HiLo can be half empty so, even if you turn up with a group of eight or so, you'll still get a table. The last time I was here with friends on a Friday night, apart from our group, there were just four old Rastas sitting around the world's tiniest TV (perched, bizarrely, on top of the world's largest TV) watching Richard Pryor Live. But with the sound off! Bizarre, perhaps, but remember; the laws that govern other universes simply do not apply here.

Top Tip – if you're eating, dress down for the occasion – it'll be cheaper.

JAPANESE

Gashi Gashi

96 Cowley Road (01865) 200789
Open Tues-Sun 6pm-late. Disabled access
Typical meal costs around £12.00
(tapas approach to Japanese eating)
Teifhoku (i.e. set meals) also available

Almost hidden away on the Cowley Road, this authentic Izakaya restaurant owes much of its reputation to the manager, Jonathan, who lived in Japan for many years before bringing his knowledge of its cuisine back to dear old Blighty.

For newcomers he will talk you through the traditions of Sushi and Japanese eating as well as showing you how to eat the food properly. There *is* a technique.

The Sushi repertoire, amongst many other choices (including veggie) is a great, tasty deep end to jump into. A nice bit of raw eel never hurt anyone so make sure when you come here, to delve into the menu and try something a bit daring.

Give yourself plenty of time for an enjoyable night ahead and try not to get too carried away drinking their Japanese beer, tempting though it is.

With all food purchased from source and all Japanese ingredients imported, you can rest assured that this is the real McCoy.

Red Star Noodle Bar

187 Cowley Road (01865) 251248
Open 6pm-11pm (no reservations)
Red Star Ramen (their specialty - £6),
Yasai Yaki Soba (veg - £4.50)

Red Star brings a communal feel to eating Chinese and Japanese food. Simply arrive and sit at a bench. The busier it is the more likely you will be seated between total strangers (something I quite enjoy) while munching through your curry, stir fry or big bowl of soup noodles. The food is delicious and inexpensive and the service quick. There's a good selection of meat, fish and veg dishes (I recommend the chicken katsu bento), which you can order as snacks (side dishes) or as mains (noodle or curry dishes). The benches lend a slightly functional/minimalist feel to eating and there's no music, which adds to overall charm.

KURDISH

Euphrates

128 Cowley Road (01865) 205204
Open weekends 6.30pm-12.30pm &
weekdays 6.30-10.30pm (later if busy)
Belly-dancing Thursday to Saturday
All main dishes around £10 before
side-dishes are added

Run by charismatic owner, Sherko, (whose claim to fame is that he once starred in a Bond movie) Euphrates offers good quality traditional food, such as Kurdish kebabs, Greek lamb and kalamari, with hot and cold meze for starters. Although most of the dishes revolve around lamb or chicken, there are several vegetarian options, including vegetable pastourma, Yemista and Mediterranean kebab. At around £9-10 for each meat dish, the main courses seem a touch expensive, particularly as you need to order side dishes for many of them, but the meat here really is very tender and succulent, and it can all be washed down with a glass of that good old Greek tipple, Ouzo.

Top Tips:

Come Thursday – Saturday and get to watch traditional belly dancing!
Book in advance and make sure to ask for one of the big tables near the door or by the fireplace.

Don't forget to round off the evening smoking one of their Hubble Bubble Pipes. The strawberry flavoured tobacco is a particular favourite.

LEBANESE

Al-Salam

6 Park End Street (01865) 245710
Open 12pm-12am daily
Average price £3 for a starter & £7
for a main meal

It's not the location, surly staff or 'God bless our house' sign' that make this place so popular, so I guess it must be the food. The menu runs the usual gamut of kebabs, lamb dishes and hummus, as well as a small selection of seafood and fish dishes, and a token concession to vegetarian dishes.

For the price, however, the quality is excellent and it can all be washed down (or coughed up) afterwards with a blast on the shisha (or hubble bubble).

Top tip – this is an ideal place to start the evening if you're in the mood for visiting all the clubs and bars on Park End Street.

Al-Shami

25 Walton Crescent (01865) 310066
www.al-shami.co.uk
Open 12pm-12am daily
Shish Taouk (chicken) £6.25, Veg Special £5.75

This being one of my favourite Oxford restaurants, I can safely recommend that to get the most variety and tastiness out of your Lebanese food, mix and match the number of starters from the huge list (there are 23 veggie choices alone!). The atmosphere here is refreshingly chatty and lively and the waiters seem to be forever running around like headless chickens.

Top tips –
Make sure you get an Al Shami credit card sized calendar. Very useful.

This is a great restaurant for eating with a large crowd of friends; the last time I visited there were 25 of us and it was fantastic. For birthdays, they'll also make cakes if you order.

MODERN CONTINENTAL

Blue Palms

7 South Parade (01865) 559653.
Open Mon-Sat 11am-11pm. Sun 11am-6pm
Chicken Cous Cous £10.50, Oven Baked
Aubergine £7.75, Salmon £9.95

Blue Palms is one of several popular eating establishments in Summertown, North Oxford. The pleasant, light ambiance here is complemented by a Moroccan/Mediterranean influence, from the artwork on the walls to the North African cuisine on the menu.

Branca

111 Walton Street (01865) 556111
Open 12pm-11pm Sun-Thurs and
11.30pm Fri & Sat
Pizza £8.50, Meat & Fish £8.50-13.00,
Veg £8-10.

'Another one of those places with big white plates, posh décor and food served by attractive foreign students', as a friend, Jo, recently, and rather succinctly, put it. Jericho's answer to Quod, Branca is busy and popular and offers a tasty but predictable menu of such dishes as Duck Confit, Pizza and Tiramasu in very stylish surroundings. The linguini and steaks seem to be their most popular dishes. Keep an eye out for their lunch deals.
Kids welcome.

The Cherwell Boathouse

Bardwell Road (01865) 552746
www.cherwellboathouse.co.uk
Open 12pm-2pm & 6pm-9.30pm daily
The 3-course set menu is £21.50

With its idyllic location by the river, the Boathouse is cosy, intimate, non-smoking, has no musak, and does mouth-watering food. It has a very impressive global wine list, good veggie dishes, is child-friendly and, when you book a table, it's yours for the whole night. During the summer months they put chairs and tables outside on the river's edge and, if you come here during the day, you can go punting before or after your meal. Make sure to book at least one week in advance during the summer, though.

Top Tip – it's a bit tricky to find, so, when you're coming down Banbury Road out of Oxford centre, keep your eye peeled for roads to the right 'til you see Bardwell Road and a sign for the boathouse. Follow your nose to the end of the lane and you'll find it there.

And look out for Helsinki, the restaurant manager, Nick Green's band, who play in various venues throughout Oxfordshire!

Gee's Restaurant

61a Banbury Road (01865) 553540
Open Mon-Sat 12pm-2.30pm and
6-10.30pm (Fri-Sat it stays open until 11pm)
Mains range from £11.50 (Tagliatelle & goats
cheese) to £18.95 (Chargrilled fillet steak)

Found a short way down Banbury Road, just before North Parade, this is one of Oxford's most cherished restaurants. Housed in an old-fashioned conservatory, Gee's once resembled a glorified tropical greenhouse, but now has created a spacious feel through the removal of a few plants (if you'd like to re-create a greenhouse feel simply bring along some tomatoes, watercress and climbers).

The food has a Mediterranean influence, with a variety of seafood, pasta dishes and steaks, many of which I've tried and found delicious. Gee's reputation for food is matched by its friendly service and atmosphere, when, in the evenings, fairy lights add to the magic of the place.

Merton's Bar

73 High Street, (01865) 249065
Open 12pm-3pm & 6pm-10pm daily
Meat Platter for two £21, Salad £8.50,
Salmon £9.50, Veg Dish £5.95 (side orders
extra at £2 each)

Formerly Café Boheme, a wing of the Eastgate Hotel and Jeremiah Grote's bawdy whorehouse, this bar-grill-restaurant is elegant, spacious and a popular haunt for the 'beautiful people'. Serving a refreshingly no-nonsense menu of fish, salads and grills, the quality of the food here suitably fits the price. Particularly recommended is the 'Trencher'. At just over £20 it makes an ideal platter for two and represents what they do best i.e. steak, poultry and game. Those with a sweet tooth won't be disappointed by the desert menu; they offer a good range of more traditional deserts and any place that has sticky toffee pudding on the menu gets full marks in my book, though they do tend to scrimp on the custard. Rarely busy (which I can't understand, owing to its grandeur, good food, and location) Merton's Bar is ideal for the start of a special night and who knows, their cosy bar might round off your evening too.

Quod Bar & Grill

92-94 High Street (01865) 202505
Open 12pm-11pm daily (No bookings on
Fridays, Saturdays and May Day)
Breakfast sometimes served 8-11.00am.
Tea & coffee all day.
Pizza £7-8, Steak £11, Veggie (pasta) £8

Big, chatty, spacious restaurant-cum-cocktail-bar that used to be a Barclays Bank. This is the kind of place where trendy, youngish, business people take potential clients and students their parents (provided dad's paying). The big wall-mounted paintings add a nice touch and make it feel like you're eating in the Tate, or somewhere in Soho. The food, mainly pasta, pizza and grill dishes, is typical for a restaurant of this style, though judging from the several times I've eaten here, simply does not match up to the price.

Tip – Pick a table that doesn't cramp your style and make sure you order separate veg as it isn't included with the main course, as one might expect.

Savannah Grill

17 Park End St (01865) 793793
www.savannah.co.uk
Open 7.15pm – 10.30pm Mon-Thurs,
7.15pm-11pm Fri, 8.15pm-11pm Sat,
8.15pm-10.30pm Sun
Sirloin Steak £15, Pumpkin & Goats cheese
parcel £10 (plus side dishes if you want them)

Adjoined to The Royal Oxford Hotel,
Savannah may not be veggie-friendly
but is a delight for the carnivore
(particularly the steak eater).
Furthermore, Savannah offers chic
surroundings, friendly service, and a
system whereby you can go to a
separate bar and taste various wines
(try that £200 Chateauneuf du Pape
you always dreamt of) before ordering
the house red. And the kitchen here is
on show, so, if you wish, you can watch
them cook your dinner.

Top Tip – Best to park in the train car
park if you're driving.

MONGOLIAN

The Mongolian Wok Bar

67-69 George Street (01865) 792919
Open Mon-Thurs 6pm-11.30pm,
Fri 6pm-12pm, Sat 5.30pm-12pm,
Sun 5.30pm-11pm, Set meal Sun-Wed £10
per head, Thurs-Sat £12; eat as much as you
like for two hours

If you like cooking, but none of the
concomitant hassle then the Wok Bar is
the perfect place for you. Simply choose
your ingredients, place them in a bowl
and hand over to someone else to
cook. Wait five minutes, collect it and
eat. Repeat this process as many times
as you want, or can manage.

The serve-yourself section contains
bowls with all kinds of veggie and meat
staples, alongside chilli, garlic and soy
sauces. The art is to get the mix right
and that's where the suggested menus,
hanging down in front of you, come in
very useful. Veggies can have their

dishes cooked in foil, so meaty oils
don't merge into their carrot stir-fries.

There is also karaoke Friday and
Saturday, starting at about 10.30pm. The
Mongolian style of low-pitched nasal
humming is not compulsory, but might
win you an admiring audience if you
attempt Bohemian Rhapsody.

MOROCCAN

Kazbar

25-27 Cowley Road (01865) 202920
Open 12pm-11pm daily
£2.50-£4.50 per dish (see below)

A bungee-jumping guitar greets you as
you enter this tastefully decorated
Morrocan tapas restaurant. The
delicious menu derives from a mixture
of Arabic and Spanish influences, with
favourite dishes including Ibikha
(chickpeas) and Albondigas (meatballs).
From the furniture to the food, it all
works very well, but can work out
expensive at £2.50- £4.50 per dish as
you'll need at least three or four each
to fill you up. Kazbah never fails to
induce a laid-back, chatty atmosphere,
so, if you're stuck for somewhere to
take that new date, this is the place for
you – find an intimate table and get
cosy! Excellent service.

SLOVAKIAN

Moya

97 St Clements (01865) 200111
Open 11am-11pm daily, Sun 11pm-10.30pm
Goulash £7.50, Venison Madallions £10.50

Don't be put off if, like me, you have no idea what to expect from a Slovak menu. This restaurant/bar offers friendly, efficient service and the hosts, Richard and Ivona, (guess which comes from Slovakia) are very accommodating, so when it comes to ordering, you'll have all the support you need. The food is, in fact, excellent, particularly the goulash, trout and Segedin (pork/ cabbage combo), and some dishes come accompanied with delicious, light, fluffy dumplings. If you're feeling adventurous, try the Ox tongue dish.

I like the relaxing ambience here and also the fact that the owners encourage the Slovak/East European community to come together through special nights on the first Sunday of each month – everyone is welcome to try more traditional Slovak dishes

NB. I like their cocktails even more than their community building project!. Moya provides a good alternative to the other excellent, though more conventional, restaurants (Fishers, Cocos) near by.

'The great soups... Venison Medallions, Slav style, delicious'
Antony Jones; The Guardian **MOYA**

Your starter for 10, what is the capital of Slovakia ?

BRATISLAVA !

Sorry, it's actually MOYA in St Clements Clearly it's time to mis-spend some of your youth there !

Opened in the summer of 2002, Moya has a contemporary, bright and clean style, it's 50% non smoking and offers the unique combination of an extensive cocktail bar with the fresh flavours of wholesome Slovak home cooking.

97 St Clements, Oxford (01865) 200111

SPANISH

Al Anduras

(01865) 516688
10 Little Clarendon Street
Open 7 days from 11am-12am
Paella £26 for two people

This cosy and popular Spanish tapas bar offers a friendly atmosphere and a wide variety of various hot and cold tapas. While the food isn't anything out of the ordinary (but let's face it – is any Spanish food?) it is ideally located and, if you're learning Spanish, provides a nice opportunity for speaking the lingo and making a fool of yourself all at the same time. Sangria carafes available.

THAI

Bangkok House

42a Hythe Bridge Road (01865) 200705
Open 5.30pm-11pm, Mon-Sat, closed Sunday
Main dish £7.00

Large, busy and well-received, Bangkok House is an all-round delight. Come here and lap up its airy décor, regal presentation and tasty Thai food. The attentive service is second to none and, if you needed any further incentive, Cliff Richard and Paul Weller have eaten here (though not together)

and there are pictures to prove it. A perfect restaurant for a 'first date'.

Top Tip – The starters are excellent, in particular, the mushroom and galangal soup which may take you to the heights of ecstasy. If you do, there are complimentary tissues in the bathroom.

Chiang Mai

130a High Street (01865) 202233
Open 12pm-2.30pm & 6pm-11pm daily
Typical main meal £7.00

If you're passionate about Thai food, this is the place to come. Chiang Mai is centrally located in a beautiful Tudor building with a lively ambience. Starters and main courses are both generous in portion and cooked with great attention. Probably a good idea to book a table.

Top Tip – Chang Mai can be tricky to find, so, if you are looking down the High Street from Carfax, keep an eye out for their sign – it's down a little alleyway to your right.

Oxford Thai

Cowley Road (01865) 203763
Open 5pm-10.30pm daily
Typical main course – meat £5.95,
prawns £6.50, veg £5.40

Like Rice Box across the road, this is not a place you'd come to linger of an evening, but, if you're on the move and want a healthy, quick, sit-down meal, it's another welcome antidote to the Friday night kebab. Offering an extensive menu and palatable food, all the place really needs is someone with a creative mind to shake off its B&H café décor and to persuade them to stop playing the likes of Alanis Morissette.

Five points if you spot its Ronnie-Biggs look-alike owner, who can be found most evenings skulking around and sucking on a fat cigar.

SOMEWHERE SPECIAL

Crazy Bear

Bear Lane, Stadhampton (01865) 890714
Open 12pm-3pm & 7-10pm (bar),
7pm-10pm daily, Sun Thai 4-10pm,
English 12pm-3pm
Thai: £20 –30 set meals,
English: 2 courses £26

This renowned hotel/restaurant on the outer skirts of Oxford has both Thai and English restaurants on its premises so, when you've finished your tempura soup and red curry, you can pop next door for treacle sponge pudding. Although I've only had a starter here, the food looks delicious and the place has an impeccable reputation. Book in advance.

Rosamund the Fair

Tooleys Boatyard, Banbury Museum,
Banbury (01295) 278690
Open Fri and Sat, 7.30pm cast off
Sun lunch 12.30pm cast off
£52 a head

Run by salty sea dog, Tim Matthews, for over 13 years, this is probably Oxfordshire's most romantic restaurant. For a sum that wouldn't break the bank (but might mean a couple of weeks in) you get a two-hour cruise through the canals and rivers of Banbury centre, with a choice of English and French cuisine freshly cooked on board.

Ideal for groups of twos and fours, the atmosphere inside is extremely intimate as the boat only seats 24, and, for the devilishly romantic men among you this is the ideal place to take the girlfriend to pop the big question. And ladies, if you want to woo him into buying you a new dishwasher, the same applies.

Closed Jan 1st - Feb 13th, when it becomes a children's roller disco.

VEGGIE & ORGANIC

The Magic Café

110 Magdalen Rd (01865) 794604
Open Mon-Sat 10am-6pm

This aptly-titled veggie café is a very popular spot for Oxford's New Age/ Hippie community, Pagan groups, political activists, goatee bearded Guardian readers, and other assorted Cowley Road residents. Find a Daily Mail reader amongst this lot and win a prize. The food is delicious, healthy, and exactly what you'd expect; a tantalising range of salads, quiches, herbal teas and mouth-watering cakes. The meals are usually around a fiver and they even produce their own cookbook, written by its owner.

Top Tip – Unless you have children yourself, you may want to avoid this place on early afternoons, as it can get a little overrun with the little blighters.

Le Manoir aux Quat' Saisons

Church Road, Great Milton, nr Oxford
(01844) 277201
www.manoir.com
Breakfast – Mon- Sun, 7.30 am-10 am
Luncheon - Mon- Sun, 12.15 pm-2.45 pm
Dinner - Mon- Sun, 7.15 pm-9.45 pm
Main Dish £32. Desert typically £18 and cheese is a very reasonable £17!
Typical night out – £200

Well, what can I say? Not a lot, as it turns out, as I've never been able to afford a night out at Le Manoir. So, to give this review some credence, I've enlisted the help of some friends who've been there. Francesco and his girlfriend, Victoria, visited in early 2003 and had 'an amazing meal and a spectacular night'. Fran said, *"We got very full and had to watch our manners"*. Full, no doubt, on Raymond Blancs veg, grown on site in their two-acre organic garden.

What about the food? Well, you can have Suprême de canette de Trelough rôti, gratin de navets et jus de canard lié au foie gras *(duck with a little bit of turnip)* or Coquille St Jacques, filets de rouget et St Pierre à l'escabèche de légumes au citron vert *(fish and veg)**. This small menu sample gives you a good idea about the depth and breadth of ingredients and dishes available. There are also children and veggie options.

Quite simply, this is the place you go when you (and your better half) have something very, very special to celebrate or you have way too much money. Whichever, invite me along for the ride.

*Any inaccuracies in spelling in this review are merely a figment of your imagination

DELICATESSENS

Nellie's Deli
36 Great Clarendon Street (01865) 557824

Tucked away down the back streets of Jericho, this old deli has been run now for nearly twenty years by its Persian owner, Mr Yazdan, and sells a satisfying selection of wine, meats, cheese and spices. Those with a sweet tooth are well catered for too, as he does a mouth-watering variety of chocolates, Italian cakes, American ice cream, baklava and more besides.

Taylors
31 St Giles (01865) 558853

This well-loved (and well-used) deli can be found on the corner of St Giles and Little Clarendon Street and is stocked to the hilt with ground coffee, fresh olives, cheese, enticing cakes and there is even a sandwich bar for tasty lunchtime nibbles. It's all a bit over-priced, but then, if you overspend here, there's always St Giles café nearby where you can binge on a week's worth of carbohydrates for under £4.

Ali's *(Lebanese Deli)*
168 Cowley Road (01865) 454010

Good selection of Lebanese dishes including Batat Harra (spiced potato dish) and Tabouli.

SPECIALIST FOOD

Eastern Continental Stores
(Indian Supermarket)
Cowley Road, opposite Tescos

Russian Fairytale *(Deli)*
88 Cowley Road (01865) 250819

A bizarre assortment of tinned foods with unknown contents, Russian dolls, music, Vodka (45 different brands!), books, sweets and my favourite – pickled gerkins (for eating with Vodka). I'd also highly recommend their Russian beer selection. There's also a small fresh food counter.

Lung Wah Chong
(Chinese Supermarket)
Hythe Bridge Road, 10am-7pm daily

Fasta Pasta *(Italian deli)*
121 Covered Market. (01865) 241973

LATE NIGHT EATING

Bodrum Kebabs
242 Cowley Road (01865) 249981
Open Mon-Sat 11am-2am-ish, Sun 1pm-2am

The best veggie kebab in the world if sampled after a ten-hours drinking marathon down the Cowley Road, but then, you'd probably feel the same about your shoes, were they lightly grilled and garnished with coriander.

Peppers
84 Walton Street (01865) 310044
Open Sun – Thurs 5.30-11.30pm,
Fri/Sat 5.30-12pm. 12.15-2pm Mon- Sat

Popular burger joint in Jericho with a good selection of sauces.

CHINESE

The Rice Box and Red Star Noodle Bar (see Chinese restaurant section)

INDIAN AND LEBANESE

Al Shami
25 Walton Crescent. (01865) 310066
Great food, but you miss out on the atmosphere of the restaurant.

Aziz
228-230 Cowley Road (01865) 794945
Excellent food, but sadly they don't deliver.

Dhaka
186 Cowley Road. (01865) 202011/200203.
Delivery 6-mile radius coverage from Cowley Road. 10% discount if collected. Free bottle of wine if spend over £25. Cheaper than Aziz but still good quality and with free salad.

Uddins Manzil
123 Walton Street. (01865) 556153
Great quality.

PIZZA

Mario Pizzeria Trattoria
103 Cowley Road (01865) 722955
Restaurant and takeaway.

Pizzas-2-Go
37 Park End Street (01865) 790606

KEBAB VANS
Price of a doner kebab varies from £3-£4

Found all over the city from the High Street all the way to St Giles and open till late (especially at weekends). Particularly well-loved by the University students, some of whom form strong allegiances with particular vans and will defend their honour to the death.

Watering Holes

What Oxford might lack in the way of nightclubs, it makes up for in its pubs. From the exotic allure of Freud's wine bar to the tiny, tumbledown, lop-sided wardrobe that is The Bear, the city is a drinker's paradise. If you're looking for pubs with a bit of style, character or history, simply avoid George Street and you can't go far wrong. After all, many of these places have been the drinking dens of famous writers, politicians and scholars for centuries. Walk into the White Horse and, chances are, that everyone from Michael Palin to Tony Blair has at some time stood on the same spot as you, ordering a pint of beer and a packet of Cheesy Wotsits.

PUBS AND BARS IN THE CITY CENTRE

The Bear

6 Alfred Street (01865) 728164
Food served every day 12pm-4pm

Tucked away, just down past the Oxford Museum, this is simply one of Oxford's most beautiful pubs, with its wooden interiors, low ceiling and outrageously uneven floors which, after too many pints, give the unwary drunk the unnerving feeling of being trapped inside a small wooden boat on a storm-tossed sea.

In summer, The Bear is an especially popular spot for post-exam revelry. Sit outside and you can soak up the party spirit, though don't be too surprised if you end up covered in eggs and flour. Also worth mentioning is the fact that they do good hearty lunches every day until 4pm, and have a long-running quiz on a Tuesday. Come and pit your wits against the professionals, as the University Challenge teams are often spotted down here practicing for the real thing. And if you're left feeling stupid after coming last, make yourself

139

feel better by challenging the weediest team member to an arm wrestle.

While some will tell you the pub's name derives from one of the symbols on the crest of the Earl of Warwick, a more fitting legend decrees that this was originally the site of a bear pit, attracting huge crowds who'd come and watch the creature dance and wrestle, until one day someone realised it was, in fact, just a particularly hairy Merton student trying to pay off his debts. So they built a pub on top of him to teach him a lesson. Probably.

What The Bear is probably best known for is its underwhelming collection of ties, which adorn the walls and ceiling. This all came about in the Fifties apparently, as the landlord, a huge Harpo Marx fan, used to carry a car horn and scissors wherever he went, and at the end of the night, after he'd had a few, would walk around blowing the horn deafeningly into the customers' ears.

Then, while they were still reeling from the shock, he'd cut their ties off and stick them on the wall. And so the collection grew to its present proportions and includes ties of such distinguished celebrities as Jeffery Archer and Les Dennis. Don't try and offer them yours though; they still have several thousand lying around in the basement.

The Eagle and Child
St Giles (01865) 310154
Food served Mon-Fri 12pm-7.45pm,
Sat-Sun 12pm-4pm

This pub has lost a bit of its magic over the last couple of years, with minor refurbishments, a fruit machine, and intrusive bland music, but you'd have to work really hard to completely spoil its charm. Like its neighbour the 'Lamb and Flag' across the road, this pub has a long literary history and has been famous as an academic haunt for many decades. Its fame derives principally from 'The Inklings', a writers'

group who used to meet here every Thursday, from the Thirties to the Sixties to discuss their work. The group consisted, amongst others, of Tolkien and C.S. Lewis, and it is said that Tolkien treated the pub so much as his second home that he kept his slippers behind the bar. The room the writers met in was called the Rabbit Room, (the area opposite the end of the bar) and, legend recalls, that after an all-day binging session on absinthe, Hugo Dyson, a member of the group, became convinced that tiny people with hairy feet were trying to steal his wedding ring. This event, of course, was to be the catalyst for Tolkien's masterpiece.

The clientele nowadays is a mix of town and gown and although it is no longer as hip as its neighbour, the pub still has some wonderful little rooms to hide away and get lost in the Lord of the Rings. The most coveted spots are the wood panelled areas by the window on the way in. The bar-food is nothing exceptional and hearing Robbie Williams blaring out utterly kills the mystique of the place, but a visit to Oxford without a pint here would be less than complete.

Gloucester Arms

Friar's Entry (01865) 241177
Food served Mon-Sun 12pm-7pm

Just behind the Oxford Playhouse this self-proclaimed Rockers' pub has DJs playing 'classic Rock and Metal' on Thursday and Friday nights, and even boasts 'the best jukebox in the world', which traverses the whole history of guitar music, from the dizzy heights of Hendrix and Led Zep to the poodle-Rock nonsense of Bon Jovi. As you can probably guess, its clientele comprises mostly Nu-Metal kids, old Rockers, Goths and Buffy fans, so why, you may

wonder, is the place decorated with wall-mounted photos of Victor Spinetti, Canon and Ball, Cilla Black, and the marvellous Bucks Fizz? There is a simple answer. This pub has the closest proximity to a theatre stage door (The Playhouse) in Britain. We measured the gap and it came to 3 feet. Regular, 'Tetley Steve', will tell you all about the actors they've had in and their colourful stories, including Nicholas Lyndhurst and his flying anecdotes and the wild drinking antics of Basil Brush. If you like Rock, actors, jukeboxes, and a nice pint, this is the place for you. If you like bland theme pubs with no atmosphere, go in the pub next door.

The King's Arms

40 Holywell Street (01865) 242369
Food served every day 11.30am-2.30pm,
5.30pm-9pm (only until 8pm Sun)

This large white pub sits on the corner of Parks Road and Hollywell Street slap-bang in the middle of town and is always very busy and popular with the University crowd. At weekends during term time, there'll always be a herd of 'Nobs' in tuxedos and ballgowns, while, during the day, you're bound to find the odd gaggle of lecturers skulking in the corners, babbling away in their own bewildering manner about convoluted theories and the price of corduroy. If you need a seat and there's nowhere to sit, show them a picture of a woman and it should be enough to frighten them away and earn you a comfy seat. The pub itself has a few interesting nooks and crannies, (especially the little rooms at the back), and is adorned with hundreds of photographs of punters past and present, as well as pictures of various members of the Royal Family doing 'common' things, e.g. Charles working the beer pumps or the Queen mum necking a pint. They also have real ales on tap and serve exceptionally average bar food.

Under-age drinking - a growing problem in Oxford

While a great pub for recording the manners, customs and social comments of the University crowd (the gents used to bear the graffiti: *'Talbot Poncenby has an arse like a wind sock'*), the King's Arms may be a bit too stuffy and unfriendly for some people's tastes. Unless you're part of the college crowd, you're probably still better off in the Turf.

The Lamb and Flag

12 St Giles (01865) 515787
Food served Mon-Sun 12pm-3pm

Formerly an old coach house, this is now one of Oxford's most attractive and convivial pubs. Even from the outside, with its narrow passageway, etched, frosted windows, and pastoral design, the Lamb and Flag seems conspiratorially inviting and has the proud claim of having been the haunt of some of the city's esteemed writers; Graham Greene wrote about it and Hardy weaved it into Jude the Obscure. In fact, the whole place has an academic dreaminess to it, especially the front part, with its wood panelling, coats of arms and low iron chandelier, giving the visitor the feeling of being enclosed in some old Victorian study.

The pub also has lots of intriguing little cubbyholes; there's one, in particular, by the bar which must have once been a cupboard, but is now a tiny one-man open cell, ideal for the solitary drinker, or anyone in need of catching up with some studying whilst soaking up the atmosphere.

Though the Lamb and Flag is almost exclusively an academic bar, don't worry about feeling like an outsider; it's very welcoming. The best time to come is early evening (before the masses pack it out), when you can find a table, linger over a drink or two and settle back with a good novel or, better still, write one. It even has its own smell; hamster cages and old woodlands. Bloody marvellous.

Next Door

38 Holywell Street (01865) 203536
www.nextdoor.tablesir.com

Formerly Blackwell's old music shop, this bar (and restaurant) is swanky, spacious, elegant, and quite new to Oxford. Open-planned and split into three levels, in the centre, by the bar, there's an octagonal glass feature with mood lighting that changes according to how close Jeremy Paxman is to the venue. Being 'Next door' to the King's Arms, it's another almost exclusive student haunt, but, unlike its rowdy neighbour, this is not the sort of place where you're going to have to spend the night standing up in a cramped space, spilling beer down your front every time someone barges past you. Plus you won't be trapped in the back room having to endure a group of Wadham students recount brash tales of their sexual conquests in loud, braying voices. Sorry, this review was meant to be about how pleasant the place is, not how awful the King's Arms can be. Come and see for yourself.

The Royal Oak

Woodstock Road (01865) 310187
Food served Mon-Sun 12pm-2.30pm, 6.30pm-9pm

Yet another Oxford pub to have enjoyed a face-lift in recent years. Gone are the old regulars and the pool table, though someone *has* had the good sense to hang on to the bar billiards and the table football. Whether you belong in the 'for goodness sake I wish they'd leave old pubs alone' camp or prefer the new upbeat, stylised look of The Oak, essentially it's still the same place, with lots of different rooms and lounging areas, and is still large enough to play hide and seek in on a Friday night. One thing that has changed however is the menu. No longer offering standard pub grub, they've gone for the more upmarket angle, proffering modern continental cuisine, which, at nearly £10 for many of the main meals, is hardly pandering to its student clientele. But then, as the girl behind the bar innocently said to me, *"It's much better here now. No-one over forty comes any more, and we're getting more of the rich, city types coming in."*

Three Goats Heads

St Michael's Place (01865) 721523
Food served Mon-Fri 12pm-8pm,
Sat-Sun 12pm-6pm

While the upstairs room is decorated with frighteningly dull architectural blueprints, the downstairs bit vaguely resembles a gents' urinal, with its traditional green tiling. They've even got their 'Fire Action Plan' framed on the wall down there, which makes me wonder which dullard was left in charge of decorating the place. That aside, this is an unpretentious and popular student haunt with cheap, strong lager on tap, and a cellar bar for finishing that difficult essay on quiet afternoons. The food, dare I say it, hovers well above the quagmire of blandness dished out in most pubs here.

The Turf Tavern

4 Bath Place (01865) 243235
Food served Mon-Sun 12pm-7.30pm

One of Oxford's best-known and most cherished pubs, the Turf has, for years, maintained that delicate balance of being a huge hit with visitors and tourists whilst maintaining its singular character, host of regulars and popularity with students.

The secret location of the pub is part of its charm, as to reach the Turf, you have to pass down a gloomy alleyway (once known as Hell Passage), and, just as you start to worry that some 19th Century street urchin is going to leap out and relieve you of your handbag, you'll find yourself in a courtyard full of noise, laughter, and the enticing smell of pub grub.

The Turf is relatively small inside (though extremely cosy in winter) whereas outside it has three large seating areas, all of which seem full most times of the day in summer. The beers are reputed to be the best in Oxford, with an endless stream of new ones on tap every week to keep you on your toes, including their wonderful green beer (which looks exactly how it sounds).

If you only had an afternoon to visit Oxford, forget trawling around colleges and museums, spend it here instead, lolling around and experimenting with the beers. This is where the heart of Oxford lies.

The White Horse

52 Broad Street (01865) 728318
Food served Mon-Sun 12pm-6pm

Wedged down in Broad Street, and surrounded by colleges and Blackwell's Bookshops, this pub attracts a marvellous wealth of characters, from the sozzled staff of local bookshops to scary looking tramps (who, it generally transpires, are college lecturers). Even Paxman has been known to drop in from time to time. If you do saunter in of an evening, which I recommend, make sure to have a natter with regular Mike (easy to find – he's *always* at the bar) as he is a mine of information about the place and its eccentric customers, and will regale you with tales of such characters as Arselips (an old beardy regular whose mouth looks like a quivering cat's rectum), 'Camel Man', and 'Captain Birdseye'.

He'll even tell you about one old regular – once the porter for the Bodleian Library – who on more than one occasion, half-way through his drink would suddenly exclaim *'Oh Shit,'* and dash out of the pub, on realising he'd forgotten to lock up the library again.

The pub does some of the best beer in Oxford and, despite its diminutive size, is well worth the visit; just pray that the party of eight students by the window will bugger off soon and give up their seats.

COWLEY RD, IFFLEY RD AND ST CLEMENTS

Baba

240 Cowley Road (01865) 203011

If Habitat and Muji got together to design a bar, this would be it. Decorated in chrome and copper, with huge mirrors and sprawling leather seating, the atmosphere is intimate, relaxed, and conducive to a good natter. Attracting a slightly older, more discerning crowd than its competitor Bar Baby, this place really is worth the trek up the Cowley Road.

Bar Baby

Cowley Road (01865) 202506

Once an antidote to the rough-and-ready pubs in the Cowley area, this place is now just one of many amongst the growing number of designer bars on the Cowley Road which seem to cater almost exclusively for a very young crowd. At the time of reviewing, however, it did have one unique and slightly controversial feature; pole-dancing. Come on a Sunday evening and watch scantily clad men or ladies getting fresh with a long, thin tube of metal. Well it makes a change to 'Songs of Praise' I suppose.

The Brickworks

182 Cowley Road (01865) 245999
Food served Mon-Sat 12pm-6pm

This was, for many years, a late-night drinking den, until one day someone turned up expressing an interest in taking *a look* at the 'late license', upon which there was much staring at the floor, shuffling of feet and clearing of throats.

Despite having reverted back to 'normal' pub hours, the Brickworks continues to be a charming, intimate, no-frills boozer, full of Cowley Road characters. Come of an evening and meet its chilled-out, friendly barman AJ or regular, 'Swiss Dave'.

Keep a look out, too, for the Kent Shrine above the bar. And thank god they've finally got rid of the tacky brick motif (with the exception of the loos).

And should you find AJ propping up the bar, fag in hand, with a wistful look in his eye, staring out onto the Cowley Road, it's only because he hasn't left the place for five years. Someone do the poor man a favour and take him out, for goodness sake, even if it's only a visit to the Bombay Emporium or for a drink over the road, at the Corridor.

The Chester Arms

19 Chester Road
(01865) 243203
Disabled toilets
Food served Mon-Sun 6.30pm-8.30pm
in winter, and lunchtimes in summer

At the end of Chester Road, just off the Iffley Highway lies this little-known pub, offering conviviality, live music, real ale and a good beer garden in summer. For friendliness it knocks the socks off all the other pubs on the Iffley Road. With a decidedly homely feel to it, it's the

Sparky shows off his new wig at the Half Moon

The Fir Tree
Iffley Road
Food is served until 9pm every night

Worth a mention for its décor alone, as this must be one of the most striking pubs in Oxford, resembling, as it does, a split-level 'funhouse' decorated by an acid-riddled obsessive collector of retro junk. With table football in the tiny backroom, bikes, records and old tin adverts on the walls; and the upside down record players on the ceiling, it is, as a friend suggested, 'designer higgledy-piggledy', and wears it well.

Popular with sporty students and friendly sozzled locals, it's a good spot for a mid-week pint and a frenzied game of table football, which is free once you've left a £2 deposit behind the bar for the ball.

The Half Moon
17 St Clement's St
(01865) 247808

This place is the latest refuge for legendary landlord Joe Ryan and his loyal following of drunken Irishmen, who have, over the years, given life and colour to various boozers up the Cowley Road, from the Bully to the Elm Tree.

A 'spit and sawdust' pub full of character and characters, the time to experience the Half Moon at its most flamboyant is on a Thursday nights when 'Sparky's Flying Circus' takes over. Despite what you might infer from the *'please refrain from snoring whilst musicians are performing'* sign, opposite the bar, you're unlikely to doze off during the performances. Like the Catweazle Club but ballsier, this open-mic evening offers larger than life performances from hurdy-gurdy players, poets, singer-songwriters, flautists and guitarist, all of whom, if its

perfect place for a quiet night on your own, curled up in front of their telly, or sunk into their chunky furniture with a good novel.

If it's company and entertainment you're seeking then come here for one of their many live music events, as their Blues and Jazz nights are excellent. The food here is 'bloody good', according to regular Dave (though he'll have emigrated to Australia by the time this comes out), with themed burgers (Thin Lizzy and chips anyone?) and a traditional Sunday lunch. Should you get curious about the acronym above the bar (**ITYIYMBAP**), the barstaff will be more than happy to oblige.

The Duke
78 St Clement's (01865) 438820

Since the demise of the New Inn and Temple Bar, their faithful Goth/ Indie/ rollie-smoking/ Burroughs reading crowd have chosen this place as their new hangout. Not a bow tie, camelhair coat, cardigan, or pair of Brogues between them, this lot are more likely to be discussing the latest Beck album than Henley Regatta. A haven for those wishing to escape the student rugger-bugger crowd in the pub next door.

eager compere Sparky is to be believed, are 'the best in the country'. Sparky, an effervescent individual, with more than a passing resemblance to Colin Baker, is 'probably the best performance poet in the UK right now' (according to Sparky!).

Moreover, there is a night for traditional Irish folk music, good beer and some legendary regulars such as Black Tom. Apparently he was once found with his trousers down by his ankles, a cigar up his arse, and his shit in the urinal. This is a *great* pub.

The Star

21 Rectory Road (01865) 248011

Hidden away off the Cowley Road, the Star is, for my money, one of the best pubs this side of town. Decorated with charming Christmas tree lights on the outside and cult movie posters and photos on the inside you'll get no prize in guessing that it's a popular student haunt, but, unlike such neighbours as the Temple Bar or the Corridor, the Star does not rely on giant TV screens and designer furniture for creating an atmosphere. Possessing that indefinable welcoming quality, this pub is friendly, laid-back, plays good music, and boasts the biggest and best beer garden in Cowley. It even has a nifty little pool room at the back with two tables, though on quiet weekdays, beware – it **can** sometimes get overrun by Goths and Indie kids indulging in a spot of mild foreplay.

Look out for the chainsaw man and the bizarre drawings behind the bar (the idle doodlings of deranged staff) and also brace yourself for last orders; they switch on these dazzling halogen lights which induce temporary blindness for about ten seconds, though you'll probably be so drunk by then you'll put it down to the beer.

As an alternative to a growing tide of designer bars in this area, the Star, with 'no plans **whatsoever** for change', is a veritable oasis.

Harcourt Arms

> 1 Cranham Terrace (01865) 310360
> Bar snacks are served until 10pm
> weekdays and 9pm weekends.

The combination of real ale on tap,
subtle lighting, unobtrusive music, two
open fires, board games at the bar and
a landlord who looks unnervingly like a
mad scientist, make this a cracking
Jericho local. Its clientele seem to be a
mixed bag of graduates and thirty-
somethings; not the sort of people
who start singing Roll out the Barrel
after half ten, more the kind to enjoy a
good debate. And it only really gets
busy in here at weekends, though
you'll still get a couple in the corner
engrossed in a game of Scrabble, even
on a Friday night.

Jude the Obscure

> 54 Walton Street
> (01865) 553344
> Food served Mon-Sun 12pm-9pm

Once the notoriously rough Prince of
Wales, this pub was transformed back
in 1995 by the arrival of eccentric
publican Noel Reilly – a thin, chain-
smoking, Irish intellectual, who named
it after one of the most depressing
novels in the English language, cleared
out the old crowd by subjecting them
to Radio 4, and brought in string
quartets, plays and philosophers to get
a 'bit of a debate going' amongst the
clientele. Sadly, his days here are long
gone (he now runs 'Far from the
Madding Crowd by Gloucester
Green), but, thanks to him, the Jude
remains a convivial pub, with a
satisfying number of seating areas, and
an unpretentious and genial crowd,
making it the natural choice for that
post-movie pint and discussion after a
night at the Phoenix.

COCKTAILS & AFTER HOURS DRINKING

Freud

> 119 Walton Street (01865) 311171
> *www.freudliving.com*
> Food 12pm-3pm, 6pm-10pm
> Open Mon-Thurs 11am-12am,
> Fri-Sat 11am-2am,(but after 10pm at
> weekends it's £4.50 to get in)
> Sun 11am-10.30pm

Converted from a church to a cocktail
bar countless years ago Freud's is
simply one of the most beautiful
places to eat and drink in Oxford. Of
course you could be forgiven for
thinking that parts of the building are
incredibly run-down but I think this
designer grottiness is a feature chosen
by its idiosyncratic owner (although
I've heard him described in less
favorable terms).

Unsurprisingly, the drinks here are
expensive, but the choice of cocktails
is excellent (try the Mexican Lullaby),
plus you can watch the bar-staff
showing off after months of watching
the Tom Cruise film 'Cocktail' on
freeze-frame. There's a fair range of

clientele here, but, predictably, more than your fair share of the posh end of the student market. You might hear horsey laughs from the ladies and some of the men believe themselves to be god's gift to women, but don't let them put you off, you can have a sophisticated evening here, even if you are surrounded by such riff-raff.

There's also plenty on offer in the way of entertainment, with Salsa on Sundays and live music/ DJs most nights of the week. Games lovers may be interested to know that Oxford 'Go' society meet here Tuesdays and Thursdays, around 6.30pm. You can sit down and have a game or two with them. They're a bit nerdy, but harmless enough.

Beware weekends here – it can get outrageously busy. It's always better to start your evening at Freud's with a cool cocktail and a seat, rather than to turn up at 10pm, when you'll have to battle the crowds and endure the braying of drunk yuppies.

Love

3 King Edward St
(01865) 200011
Open 5.30pm-1am Fri-Sat

Cool, modern and sexy, this is poles apart from the stuffy pubs and restaurants found on and off the High Street and must have come as a welcome change for the students here too. Cocktails here are, naturally, de rigueur. Downstairs there's a dance area, a lap-dancing pole (unused so far), little cubicles you can hide away in with friends, and even mixed sex toilets where women get the chance to discover what men talk about behind closed doors (nothing) and men finally get to discover what the ladies talk about (everything).

Allegedly, they got their license by opening as a restaurant, but as the only thing on the menu is a curry at £100, I reckon their chefs have a rather easy time of it. Good scam.

Raouls Cocktail Bar

32 Walton Street
01865 553732
www.raoulsbar.com
Mon-Thurs 4pm-12am, Fri-Sat 4pm-1am,
Sun 4pm-12am

Knock, knock
Who's there?
Two blokes
You're not coming in.

Any club/ bar that operates such fascistic weekend door policies as Raoul's would not normally receive my custom, particularly after having found myself on the receiving end last time I tried to get in with a friend to review the damn place. It seems that, at weekends, Raoul's knuckleheaded bouncers keep a tally of male and female numbers, and if it all gets a bit too male-heavy inside, they try and redress the balance by stopping any men coming in, unless accompanied by an **equal** number of women. So, it's couples or women only for as long as it takes to harmonise the ratio, while the boys are left standing around outside, waiting until their presence inside is deemed necessary. Now, in my book, **nobody** should ever be made to feel inferior by the idiotic door policies of an insignificant wine bar and I'd happily support an embargo on such places. And, just one last thing (then I promise to stop ranting) - would they operate a similar policy if there were too many women inside?

For those who don't wish to heed my advice, what can I tell you? – it's insanely popular with students, is a paean to the colour brown, and its owners probably aspire to having Posh and Becks drink here.

Now, where did I leave my handbag?

Thirst

7 Park End Street
(01865) 242044
Open Mon-Sat 5pm-1am

Designer bar for young clubber types, with University students mixing alongside locals and DJs twiddling away on Friday and Saturday nights. Rather like Love, but here the skirts are shorter, the heels are higher, and the boys rather over-do it on the hair-gel.

And if you're really desperate...

There are also several eating places along the Cowley Road that serve as convenient after-hours drinking establishments for the boozed-up desperados. Ask around and you'll find out where they are.

UNIVERSITY BARS

Most University bars are a sorry state of affairs, and with so many wonderful pubs in Oxford, you'd be chomping at the bit after spending the night in one of these dingy caverns. Saying that, there are a few exceptions, notably New College, Wadham and Magdalen. Wadham is great in summer as the bar spills out onto the lawns; Magdalen is very beautiful and has a riverside terrace, and New College is proud of its Wurlitzer jukebox. If you're not a University member you're more likely to sneak in on weekdays, as most weekends there'll be some sort of ticket policy or a bouncer, who, if he doesn't like the look of you, will require you to quote from The Iliad – extensively, and in Greek – to get past him.

OFF THE BEATEN TRACK

The Isis Tavern
Iffley Lock, Iffley Village

With an expansive garden overlooking the river, and being only accessible on foot from Donnington Bridge or via Iffley lock, the Isis Tavern has always had the potential for being one of Oxford's most beautiful pubs. Instead, it's a run-of-the mill chain pub with TV screens, continuous chart music and a naff sporty theme. This used to be my local many moons ago and I still get mildly depressed every time I remember how it used to be. Gripes aside, they offer standard pub-grub, and offer mulled wine and a real fire in winter. And, if you're ambling down the lock one summer's afternoon and fancy a little refreshment, it makes a welcome break.

Traditionally the architecture students from Brookes University have their results pinned up on the tree in the centre of the beer garden every year, though I've never found out why.

Prince of Wales
73 Church Way, Iffley Village
(01865) 778543

Authentic, old-fashioned pub, complete with a Freddie Starr look-alike landlord. The food here really is very good, particularly if you love Sunday roasts. Outside, there is a pagoda at the front, and a paved, flowery bit at the back, while inside there are some big tables, ideal for large groups. For lovers of real ale it's a must; they usually have eight different types on offer every week. Situated in the heart of Iffley village, the river and lock are just a short walk away for an ideal, lunch-time pre-amble, or a midnight adventure after closing time.

The Trout

Godstow Road Wolvercote

To get here follow the Woodstock road all the way to the ring-road then take a left into Wolvercote and you can't miss it.

Boasting its fair share of unusual features, across the river on the opposite bank is a strange garden with stone lions and other odd things, while, spanning the river itself, is a dilapidated wooden bridge straight out of Tomb Raider. The pub also has two resident peacocks, Darren and Shirley, who will happily share your dinner with you, especially if you're having the pub's speciality birdseed salad.

The combination of beautiful surroundings and excellent food means that in summer, The Trout is usually packed with tourists, while during term time it seems a popular place for students to bring mum and dad. In fact the pub **always** seems busy; try coming mid-afternoon in February and you'll see.

As a consequence, it has become somewhat the victim of its own success and, despite its size, it can still be hard to get a seat, while queues for the food can be tiresome, so make sure you arrive very early lunchtime or evening. But, if you can handle the crowds, The Trout is a near-idyllic country pub, which, on a warm summer's afternoon, is a rare treat.

The Perch

Bisney Lane off the Botley Road

The younger brother of the Trout, inside it's too much fake 'olde worlde' for my liking, with stuffed fish, horse brasses and whatnot, but it doesn't matter too much, because you'll want to sit outside anyway. To reach it, go up the Botley Road past the station, look for signs to the golf course, then

Beer garden at The Perch

follow the track for ages until you find the pub at the end. During winter, it's fairly unspectacular, but, in summer, is packed with tourists.

(See parks and gardens section for how to walk to the Perch and the Trout from Port Meadow)

The Bat and Ball

(01865) 8743791 0 miles south of
Oxford High Street Cuddesdon

Opened by a cricket fanatic ten years ago, this large and attractive, country pub is eccentrically decorated with cricket posters, newspaper articles, ties, gloves and over 1000 bats (they've got Saddam Hussein's hanging above the bar). What's more, it serves its own cricket inspired make of beer: LBW. It even has a cabinet in one corner housing little golliwog figurines in cricket garb, which when spotted recently by the owner of the Inner Bookshop (out having his Sunday lunch), caused him to choke to death on his vegetarian quiche.

And, on the subject of food, the Bat and Ball does a terrific pub lunch, with plenty of pies, fish and steak on the menu, and burgers specially made by the local butchers in Watlington. It's a little on the expensive side (£10+ for most meals) but how could you resist those generous helpings of chicken pie and sticky toffee pudding, all washed down with a pint of beer?

Despite being only fifteen minutes drive from the city centre, the Bat and Ball really is out in the sticks – ideal if you need to walk off that heavy lunch in pleasant, rural surroundings. If you do take a wander, you might happen to pass the famous nearby ecclesiastical Ripon College, which explains why the pub is so often full of pissed men, with side-partings, discussing theology.

If it's a tourist-free and charming country pub you're after, with decent grub and a signed photo of Fred Trueman, look no further.

Discotheques

Considering the enormous student population at the University and Brooke's, the local population, and all the tourists that visit this town, the club scene in Oxford has always been something of an embarrassment. With most clubs here still erring more towards the Grange Hill school disco than the Big Beat Boutique, you might think you'd be best off staying at home with a copy of Ibiza Anthems '92 and drinking Kestrel lager.

In the last few years, however, with the refurbishments at the Bully and Zodiac down the Cowley Road, and places like Po Na Na and The Bridge opening up in town, Oxonians have finally begun to realise there is more to clubbing than waving your arms around to 'Dancing Queen'.

So who knows, maybe one day in our lifetime a new dawn will come when Oxford will have the capacity for tempting out even the most eclectic audiophiles for a night of serious clubbing. In the meantime, if you're looking for cheesy chart music, mirrored ceilings and somewhere to swing your handbag, welcome to paradise.

The Bridge

Hythe Bridge Street (01865) 242526
www.oxfordevolution.com

A more recent addition to the glut of banal clubs in the city centre, the Bridge is busy, spacious (two floors and a pretty big dance area) and particularly popular with students during the week when it's cheaper. While taking itself more seriously than some of Oxford's cheesier clubs, and certainly more stylish, it's still essentially another cavernous meat-market with over-priced drinks and nowhere to sit.

The Backroon at the Bully

162 Cowley Road (01865) 244516

Back in the dark ages, the Bully was a fabulous spit and sawdust Irish pub, with a beer garden at the back that was essentially a rubbish tip with old tyres, crates and a broken down van. Those days are long gone and now the back room is host to a variety of gigs and club nights that range from Trance/Dance to Indie.

Don't get your hopes up too much about the venue itself; it is literally the back room of a pub that any experienced clubber would turn their nose up at, but the friendly loved-up crowd here are a welcoming and enticing bunch. And, most importantly, it's been blessed with that Cowley Road magic. Saying all that, the last time I was here on a Friday it was packed with the over-fifties. You may have been warned.

Club Latino

St Clement's Street (01865) 247214

Akin to the first two circles of Dante's inferno, Club Latino is where foreign students and sleazy men are sent to pay penance for their fashion mistakes. While the top circle is a cold and lifeless void with nowhere to sit, (except in the TV room, which always seems to be showing some Spanish soap opera), descend into the second level and your ears will pick up the torturous sound of Salsa-Europop. Down here, slip-on shoes and

Face sucking night at The Bridge

moustaches are de-rigueur (for men and women) and, again, there's nowhere to sit except a tiny booth in the corner by the bar that somehow feels like you're sitting in a urinal. Oxford's answer to a caravan site nightclub without the Status Quo covers band.

Downtown Manhattan
George Street (01865) 721101
www.dtmoxford.co.uk

Abiding by the principle that if you wait long enough you'll eventually come back into fashion, DTM has stuck determinately to its cheesy furnishings, anodyne chart music, and titchy dance floor for over 20 years now. Despite a recent renovation (they changed the carpet), the dance floor is still ridiculously small and the DJ's habit of playing about 30 seconds of a song before launching into another is bloody annoying. But, with half the couples up on the dance-floor practising their Dirty Dancing routine and slobbering in each other's ears, its best avoided anyway. The clientele, too, are a strange bunch, ranging from virgin clubbers, lager boys, and older women on the pull, to Tarquin and chums, in their chunky jumpers, on the look out for 'totty'.

Of all the nightclubs in Oxford, this is one of them.

Park End
37-39 Park End Street (01865) 250181

Oxford's largest club, attracting stag and hen parties in their droves, and the type of punters for whom size is everything. With three big dance floors and a huge capacity, it does, however, attract the occasional big-name DJ and the likes of Ministry of Sound. And a £1 million makeover in recent years means the club now has better air-

conditioning, 6 bars, a new dance-floor and improved decor.

That aside, it's still horribly tacky and the mid-week student nights are probably the best times to come if you really have to. Its popularity means you will invariably be queuing outside for a while, which, if you are male, is a golden opportunity to get into an argument and possible fight with some bloke who takes offence to the way you were looking at his girlfriend.

Po Na Na Souk Bar
13-15 Magdalen Street (01865) 249171
Open 9pm-2am

With a Moroccan touch to its decor, Po Na Na (named after the wombat in the Lion King) has a cool dance floor and two bars serving bottled beer and cocktails. A hip town and gown crowd happily mix in the various nooks and crannies, while others just seem to come here to get some kip in the bed just by the dance floor. Waiting for drinks is never too much of a problem here but you could be queuing outside for a while, especially at weekends, if you arrive after pub closing. There also seems to be a fairly strict door policy regarding big groups of lads, so, if there's a bunch of you, it's best to turn up in twos and threes. The music varies throughout the week, from Jazz-Funk beats to guest DJs. Probably the best club in central Oxford.

The Zodiac

190 Cowley Road (01865) 420042
www.thezodiac.co.uk

Starting life as The Co-op Hall, this was a venue where, back in the bad old days, you'd have to slip down a shabby alleyway then up some stairs into what looked like an old school hall to see bands struggle through a crap PA. Nowadays the corridor has gone, the PA is top notch, and it's a bit cleaner, but the school hall remains – host to different bands and club nights throughout the week.

As a music venue the Zodiac is pretty good, being more intimate and cheaper than most London venues and often attracting plenty of big name bands for warm up gigs before their major tour. On busy nights though, be ready for a lonnnnnggg wait at the bar.

The Downstairs Bar usually has a different thing going on to upstairs, and has a sort of Gaudi look corner bar where you can escape the sheer volume of the music and actually have a chat.

Club nights here are of varied quality and range from Indie to Hard House. Wednesday's Fuzzy Ducks is renowned as a shag-fest for students. They all pile in, get a drink from the bar, then start grabbing. It's like musical chairs, except the one left at the end is the loser. Described by FHM as the *'easiest shag in the country'.*

Unlike most other clubs in Oxford, the Zodiac mercifully doesn't appeal to the stereotypical town crowd who like nothing better than wearing swimwear in sub-zero temperatures and rounding off the evening with a good scrap. Instead, with its mix of students and Cowley Road regulars, the club is friendly, flirty, and one of the best nights out you can have in Oxford.

And, finally, while you're reaching for your disco clobber, a bit of good old fashioned parental advice –
If you hand your coat in at the cloakroom try everything in your power to collect it ten minutes before the end, as, after 2am, the service is appallingly slow. And, if you lose your ticket as I did last time I was there, then, god help you, the kebab vans will be long gone before you finally escape.

Ententainment

THEATRE

Apollo Theatre
George Street (01865) 243041
www.cc.live.co.uk
Ticketmaster 0870 606 3500

This 1930s theatre, designed with the rather surreal theme of Tutankhamun crossed with Italian street theatre, plays host to the typical big budget stuff, offering everything from West End musicals to boy bands, 60s revival bands and big-name comedians. Even wrestling has been on the bill recently.

No theatre is complete without its ghosts and the Apollo is no exception. In fact there was an attempt, by visiting psychic Derek Acorah, to exorcise its three resident ghosts, Helen, Jim and Jack, only a few year ago. Though Derek provided the necessary ritual of mumbling, going red in the face and waving his hands about, Jim, it seems, refused to budge. According to legend, it that his cold presence can still be felt in the top circle, especially when the Chuckle Brothers are performing.

The Burton-Taylor Theatre
Gloucester Street (01865) 798600
www.burtontaylor.co.uk

This seasonal, student-run theatre puts on a feisty selection of contemporary drama, comedy and new writing from students and the local community. This is modern, amateur theatre at its most intimate and best.

The Old Fire Station
George Street (01865) 794494

180 capacity theatre with a predictable selection of mainstream fodder from Shakespeare to Pinter. Sort of the baby brother of the Apollo. The downstairs room is café-bar by day and club by night, and should be approached with extreme caution.

Pegasus Theatre
Magdalen Street (01865) 722851
www.pegasustheatre.org.uk

Starting life as a converted school canteen 30 years ago, the Pegasus is now a centre for youth arts, contemporary dance, music, mime and underground theatre. The shows are usually a mix of locally based youth productions and more underground professional touring companies. During the week they run youth workshops where potential luvvies can learn lighting, sound or stage management skills.

Legend has it that, on Halloween at the stroke of midnight, the ghosts of the old dinner ladies can be seen wandering around smelling of boiled cabbage and soya mince. To free them from their nocturnal wanderings, a virgin drama student has to kiss their stubbly chins then polish off second helpings of mashed potato.

The Oxford Playhouse

Beaumont Street (01865) 305305

Usually this is the kind of place you'll see Prunella Scales doing Chekhov or Judy Dench doing David Hare but they also put on everything from poetry slams to comedy, lectures and musicals. Not quite as grand as the Apollo but mercifully less mainstream.

Drama at the University

Many of the colleges stage theatre in the summer season. Some, like Wadham, have their own theatres, while others will mount performances in their gardens and quads, weather permitting. Most colleges advertise on boards outside their entrances and on posters around town. Failing that, Tourist Information give details of daily performances throughout the year. Though students tend to stick to fairly traditional stuff like Shakespeare and Marlow, on a warm summer's evening this form of theatre can be a sublime experience, even if your King Lear is a skinny 18 year old with bum-fluff.

Outdoor theatre with Creation Theatre Company

June-September (01865) 250636/ 245745
enquiry@creationtheatre.co.uk
www.creationtheatre.co.uk

In the past Creation Theatre used to perform within the grounds of Magdalen College School, but have recently moved to the equally beautiful Headington Hill Park (see parks and gardens). Outdoor theatre doesn't come more magical than this, with the company intelligently making use of their surroundings whichever way they can. Previous productions have seen actors abseiling from trees, arriving in boats, declaiming from tree houses, and, occasionally, falling in the river.

The company perform two plays each summer, usually 6 times a week. It's nearly always Shakespeare, though they do occasionally branch out and once did a stunning version of 'Alice Through the Looking Glass', with the audience following Alice on her adventures around different parts of the island.

Evening performances vary in time, usually between 7-8pm, but it's best to contact the box office for details. This is an event not to be missed.

Hi there. Im a young Kim Basinger and I would like to tell you about the fun you can have at the PHOENIX PICTURE HOUSE in Oxford. Because they show the best in world and indie cinema you are virtually guaranteed to see either a womans front bottom or a mans dingler dangler on the big screen.
Cafe | Bar
late night flicks
fab membership scheme
www.picturehouse-cinemas.co.uk
PHOENIX Picture House Oxford
57 WALTON ST
BOOKING LINE (01865) 512526
24 HR INFO (01865) 554909

CINEMA

From Art-house cinema to the Hollywood blockbusters, Oxford can cater for all your celluloid needs. Here's how.

Maison Francaise
Norham Road   (01865) 274220
maison@sable.ox.ac.uk

If you're a lover of French cinema you might be interested to know that, every Monday during term-time at the Phoenix cinema, Maison Francaise shows a range of subtitled contemporary and classic French films ranging from Godard to Jeunet and Caro. Free to language students.

For more details, consult the Phoenix programme.

Odeon
Magdalen Street and George Street
0870 5050007

I can't quite figure out the need for two similar cinemas a stone's throw from each other, but they seem to do

well, so why grumble? George is like the younger of two brothers who gets all the hand-me-downs after Magdalen has done with them.

The Phoenix
57 Walton Street, Jericho
(01865) 554909/ 512526 (for booking)
www.picturehouse-cinemas.co.uk

Built in the 1910s, this cinema in the heart of Jericho has had a long and colourful life, particularly during the 1970s, when, as La Scala, it showed nothing but porn. Nowadays, the Phoenix is a popular Art-House cinema, running everything from the latest Jim Jarmusch to cult classics, and any sweaty men in raincoats you might still spot here are most likely to be just physics students taking an evening off.

The cinema also has a cafe-bar upstairs, where you can hang-out and talk movie-trivia, while, on the ground floor you might want to make use of the suggestion box, as they may agree to show a movie you've been dying to see for years. The Phoenix even occasionally plays host to directors who, after their new film has been shown, will appear to take questions from the audience.

Immensely popular and by far the best cinema in Oxford, it is advisable to book, especially at weekends, when they also show late-night, cult flicks.

The Ultimate Picture Palace

Jeune Street (01865) 245288

This place used to show old classic B-movies and cult films, but, nowadays, seems mainly to show the more independent stuff that was out just a few months before. The UPP is far from being in the best of health, but, I guess, its seedy run-down look is all part of the charm.

Once the *Penultimate* Picture Palace, it used to have these giant Al Johnson hands hanging above it, but, one day, two of the fingers fell off, leaving Al giving the two-finger salute to the Cowley Road and so the hands were discreetly removed.

Catweazle Club

Northgate Hall St Michaels St, every Wednesday
Contact *mattsage1@hotmail.com*

Having been running now for countless years, the Catweazle Club is, quite simply, something of a legend in Oxford. A platform night for local talent, some of the musical performances here can be quite stunning, while the line-up each evening is usually eclectic enough to take in everything from singer-songwriters, lute-players, and demon fiddlers to storytellers, performance poets, and even duelling trombonists! If you fancy trying out your latest poetic masterpiece or singing a sea-shanty, these guys will make you feel very welcome (although I do think charging performers an entrance fee seems a little mean-spirited). The club is run by the very charming and enthusiastic Matt Sage, and the room is

Matt welcomes on stage the world's tiniest man

thoughtfully decorated with lots of lovely touches, from subtle lighting to cushions on the floor and flowers on the stage. The atmosphere can be quite intimate and magical at times but it does get busy after 9.30pm, so try and get there for 9pm if you want a seat.

As a warning, this is not everyone's cup of tea; the audience can only be described as a mixed bag of eco-friendly New-Agers, earnest old hippies, beautiful arty types and blokes in wellies, and the atmosphere sometimes can seem a little 'worthy'. If you're cynical, or the kind of person who hates jugglers, you probably won't like this place either. But if you can overcome your prejudices, or if you fancy performing, I can guarantee you'll have a terrific evening here. The Catweasel Club shows that the city really does have a life outside of the University. And a heartbeat too.

Jongleurs Comedy Club
3-5 Hythe Bridge Street (01865) 722437
Open Thurs-Sat until 2am every night
Student Concessions Thursday, Expensive
Popular with the mid-thirties crowd, Jongleurs comedy nights seem marketed for those people who feel too old to go to proper clubs but still want to do something different to a night down the local. Not only that, they're probably the only social group prepared to pay the steep weekend prices.

Each night three comedians perform, with the comedy usually finishing around 11pm, when the disco kicks in. For the first hour it's 80s and Disco classics, again aimed at the thirty-somethings who will dance if Loveshack or La Bamba, but might get frightened off by Eminem. After they've all gone home at 12.30am to relieve the baby-sitter, the night usually reverts to chart anthems and a bit of House.

Being part of a nationwide chain, these comedy nights are very formulaic, eliminating the element of danger that keeps comedy fresh. But, if you're partial to a bit of stand-up, or organising a stag/ hen night, you're most likely to come here on the grounds that there isn't actually anywhere else for you to go.

The Oxford Music Scene

The Oxford music scene actually kicked off in 1977 with the release of 'Romeo' by Mr. Big, but, seeing as no one seems to remember it, we'll move swiftly on. Let's say it had as much relevance to Punk as Steps and leave it at that.

Things were quiet for a few years after that, but then, in the mid-Eighties, came the brief but refreshing C86 scene, courtesy of the NME. Out went the poncy New Romantic bands, with their frilly hair and tartan waistcoats, and in came tall, skinny school-kids sporting floppy haircuts, anoraks and badly tuned Fender Jaguars, and singing songs about doing the washing-up. Tallulah Gosh were one of the few local bands to survive the scene, transforming first into Heavenly and then later intoMarine Research. The last I heard, they'd been supporting Fugazi, though this was some time back, and they might all be dentists now. The band that really did help put Oxford on the map during this period, however, was Ride.

Up until the late Eighties this pre-pubescent foursome were little more than Pet Shop Boys wannabes, but, after accidentally seeing a My Bloody Valentine gig at the Wheatsheaf, they suddenly realised that guitar noise and floppy hair was where it was at. Within a year they gave Creation Records their first top 75 hit single with the release of the seminal 'Drive Blind' EP. Inspired also by the likes of Jesus and Mary Chain and Sonic Youth, Ride found themselves at the forefront of what briefly became the Shoegazing, or 'Thames Valley' scene. This was a musical fashion that involved heavy textured guitar sounds, distant vocals, staring at your feet on stage, and the legal requirement of having been born somewhere near Aylesbury.

It was around this time, too, that local promoter, Mac, with a good ear for the next big thing, was running the Jericho Tavern and regularly featuring early Creation bands such as Primal Scream, as well as the likes of Carter USM and local band On A Friday, all of which were then playing to crowds of little more than 100.

On A Friday were the early incarnation of Radiohead, who, with Mac's help, attracted the attention of A&R guys, and it wasn't long before they were signed to a major label. The only problem was their name. The band had chosen it because they used to rehearse 'on Fridays'. I know, I know, it's hard to imagine that this is the same band whose music and lyrics only a few years later would so beautifully describe the dark paranoia and loneliness of the late 20th and early 21st Century. After much nagging from the record company they were eventually given a choice of five names and ordered to pick one by the end of the day.

The choices were:

1) The Muhammed Alis
2) Dearest and Shindig
3) A horse, a Spoon and a Bucket
4) Radiohead
5) The Desperate Tricycles

It was a tough call but they finally plumbed for Radiohead, the name deriving from a Talking Heads track on the True Stories LP.

After the worldwide success of Creep and a surprise number one in Israel, Radiohead firmly made Oxford the place to watch for the next big thing and it wasn't long before those three cheeky young whippersnappers with one enormous eyebrow caught the attention of the music press.

The Jennifers started life in the early Nineties as Ride wannabes, but, before long, they'd changed their name and their line-up and, much to everyone's relief, finally stopped putting wah-wah solos in every song,. The release of their first single, a short, but catchy, little punky number 'Caught by the Fuzz', took everyone by surprise and they were an overnight success. The band, of course, were Supergrass and, for a while, they secured for Oxford a reputation as England's foremost melting pot of talent.

On the strength of this, and with the concerted efforts of local promoters, Radio 1 brought Sound City to Oxford in 1997, and, for a short while, even Tony Blair considered packing in politics and re-forming his old Oxford band Ugly Rumour.

Without the emergence of another big name in recent years, Oxford might appear to be losing its touch, but one only has to flick through the pages of Nightshift, or pop down to the Bully or Wheatsheaf, to realise that there are still a whole host of bright young things out there waiting to spearhead a new movement in pop.

As Billy Bragg once sang, 'the revolution is only a T-shirt away.'

POP TRIVIA AND
SONGS ABOUT OXFORD

Caught by the Fuzz/ Strange Ones - Supergrass

You get two for the price of one on
Supergrass's debut single. While 'Caught by
the Fuzz' is the tale of a very young Gaz
getting nicked in Oxford for possession of
cannabis, the B-side, 'Strange Ones', pays
homage to the Cowley Road Care in the
Community Centre and all the vagrants that
hang out around Methadone Park near the
Zodiac. I've even been told that Supergrass's
first album, 'I should Coco', was inspired by
Café Coco at the bottom of Cowley Road,
but I'm not fully convinced by that one.

OX4 - Ride

The last track from their second album, 'Going Blank Again', takes its name from
the band's post-code. It's one of those songs about being away from home too
long and missing your girlfriend and your mum's cooking, complete with Ride's
trademark swirly guitars and quiet, soupy vocals.

Itchycoo Park - The Small Faces

It seems that Steve Marriot and co had been in a few dodgy dealings with
some Eastend gangsters, and to let things cool down a bit the record company
paid for a trip to Oxford to keep them from concrete slipper land. Whilst in
Oxford, it seems that the boys had a jolly nice time and, after several spliffs,
cobbled together this song. Listen out for references to the Bridge of Sighs
and Dreamy Spires.

Radiohead

Although the band did record a song in the early
days called 'Million $ question', where Thom
expresses his desire to 'ram-raid his old employers;
Cult Clothing', no subsequent material has provided
titles directly related to Oxford. Listen to the likes of
'Prove Yourself', 'Subterranean Homesick Alien', and
'Street Spirit', however, and you'll hear Thom
rhapsodising on alienation, pollution, crap housing
and god knows what else to do with the town. Oxford may get a pretty hard
time in several Radiohead songs, but they all still live here (or near by), so it can't
be as bad as all that, can it? Remember guys; LA is just a plane flight away...

Shotover Hill - Supergrass (from the album 'Supergrass')

This track appears on Supergrass's third album and name-checks a popular local spot for stoners to hang out. And, knowing Supergrass, that's probably what they get up to there, too.

Quality But Hers - Dustball

For the title of their first album on local label Shifty Disco, Dustball found inspiration from a butcher's shop on the Cowley Road. The shop used to bear the sign 'Quality Butchers' but, over time, the letter 'c' had fallen down and no one had bothered to replace it. This was an album title waiting to happen and these guys had the genius to recognise it.

Double Decker - The Bigger The God

It's about the Oxford park and ride system, apparently. And I think we've gone as far as we can with this idea.

The Beatles

Although few people know it, the Beatles did actually visit Oxford in the 1960s, owing to the labours of Jeffery Archer, who, then, was a hard-working fund-raiser for the University, rather than the low-life, talentless, jail-bird that we know him as today. Having donated a few items to the college for auction, the Beatles were duly invited by Archer to Brasenose College for dinner, and, by all accounts, everyone had a jolly nice time. It was the only time the Beatles visited the city in their whole career.

Legends in their own lunchtime

Hairo and the Biros

Formerly the Quiet Men, the Biros once performed the strangest gig I have ever seen in the basement of The Old Fire Station. The gig started well until their singer, Hairo, persecuted by his own equipment, appeared to be getting badly electrocuted by his guitar. Around the same time some bloke in the audience pulled out a bag of diced carrots and, for no good reason, started throwing them at the band.

As the carrots rained down and the electrocutions got worse, Hairo did what any self-respecting singer would do, and stormed off stage. Years later he moved to London and formed a band called 'Friends of David', a name I'm proud to say I inspired. As you can imagine, I was very keen for them to be famous as it would have made a great chat-up line, but, alas, it wasn't to be.

Arthur Turner's Lovechild

Having been fronted by the *'terrifying and bald'* local legend and promoter, Mac for well over 15 years, the band only recently called it a day, though Mac can still be found doing the odd guest spot at Your Song. Having taken their name from the former caretaker of Oxford United, ATL famously signed to Oxford's Rotator Records on the local team's pitch at half-time for the princely sum of £1.

The Bigger the God

This weird bunch have been around for countless years now, pushing their unique brand of camp, Gothic cabaret. Despite brief flirtations with fame on the Big Breakfast and Top of the Pops Two, it just wasn't to be, yet they still remain active for the sheer pleasure of playing together. And it is no small compliment that the editor of Nightshift, Dale Kattack, once described their guitarist, Ellis, as 'one of the great, unsung songwriters in the country'.

Swervedriver

Their song, 'Son of Mustang Ford', seemed to appear on every Indie compilation in the early 90s and for a short while, Swervedriver were in fashion. Since then the dreadlocks may have gone, but legend has it that the band are still on the go and recently had a top 70 hit in Papua New Guinea.

ATL show off their 1p cheque

Ronan, Mac and Dave of Shifty Disco

LOCAL LABELS & MAGAZINES

Rotator Records
www.rotator.co.uk

Set up in 1995 by local promoter and entrepreneur, Richard Cotton, Rotator signed up the likes of the Mystics, Sweeney, and Arthur Turner's Lovechild and even achieved a top forty hit with the Candyskins single, 'Monday Morning'. Rotator have remained pretty quiet recently, but, with the success of Richard's new studio on Magdalen Street, may well be on the prowl again for some new talent.

Shifty Disco
www.shiftydisco.co.uk

Set up in 1997 by the gang from Nightshift, the release of the first singles by Dustball and Nought brought instant recognition for the label, as both bands found themselves invited to perform a Peel session. From this promising start the label has grown from strength to strength releasing twelve singles and several albums every year. Previous highlights include albums from the likes of Mark Gardner (Ride), the

Unbelievable Truth, and the compilation album 'The Sounds of the Suburbs', which accompanied the Channel 4 series of the same name. Meanwhile, their spin-off label, 'Star Harbour', has been busy releasing singles and achieved a top twenty hit in 2002 with the novelty record 'The wheels of the bus', by Mad Donna.

If that isn't enough to whet your appetite, how could you resist the charm of some of their fruitier bands, such as Spinach, Pluto Monkey, Elf Power, Murry the Hump and Frigid vinigar.

Look out for their stuff in the record shops around town, particularly Polar Bear on the Cowley Road. Failing that, get yourself on their mailing list from the above address and hear some of the coolest music this side of the planet.

Truck Records
www.truckrecords.com

Set up in 1998, this label has grown from strength to strength, releasing records from the likes of Goldrush, KTB and 'Meanwhile Back in Communist Russia'. They even have their own annual festival. To find out more, visit the website.

17

Nightshift

www.nightshift.oxfordmusic.net

This free local magazine has been Oxford's bible for what's on, who's worth seeing, and all the latest news about the local band scene for what seems like 15-odd years, though my memory's not what it was, so it could be even longer. Heroically holding the Oxford band scene together, as well as organising events, Nightshift is essential reading for anyone remotely interested in keeping music live and supporting Oxford bands. If that's not enough, there's yet more information on their thoroughly entertaining website.

Favourite line from Nightshift- 'If white bread could play guitar it would sound like Shed Seven.'

Oxfordbands.com

Information on up-and-coming gigs, band profiles, record reviews, interviews, venues, recipes and more besides.

Oxfordmusic.net

This is essentially an on-line shop selling albums by everyone from Ride to John Otway. They also sell T-shirts and tickets.

Wegotickets.com

Pretty self-explanatory.

OXFORD MUSIC EVENTS

The Punt

Some time in May
Contact Nightshift for more information

Oxford's answer to the Camden Crawl, this annual music event has around 20 local bands in different venues around the city, giving it their all in one mad afternoon.

Your Song

Twice a year, around 20th August (Mac's birthday) and Christmas

This started over ten years ago at the Jericho Tavern as a bit of fun and has now become a regular twice yearly event, where the best of Oxford's local bands try their hands at a few (often outrageous) covers.

Over the years we've seen an early incarnation of Supergrass play Disney songs; Radiohead, in a moment of rare humour, perform 'Rhinestone Cowboy', 'Money' and 'Hooked on Classics'; and the sadly defunct Ultrasound condense the whole of Tommy into a twenty-minute medley, complete with full costume and ham acting.

But the band who, over the years, has contributed the most consistently stunning performances has to be local legends, The Bigger The God. Everything, from Laurel and Hardy's 'Trail of the Lonesome Pine' to Jilted John's 'Gordon is a Moron', has been attempted, and who could forget when, mid-way through singing 'My Way', singer, David, stopped, took off his Dr Marten boot and, using it as a telephone, had a chat with the late Frank Sinatra?

More recent highlights include the Young Knives performing Barbara Streisand's 'You don't bring me flowers', with their bassist, 'The House of Lords' dragged up and being serenaded by his brother. And at one Xmas event, the keyboard player from 'Rock of Travolta' got so drunk that he managed to throw up whilst singing 'Gotta get through this'.

As you can see, this is an event not to be missed. Keep checking Nightshift for details.

can get a bit uncomfortable, especially when squashed up against fat, hairy, beery Blues fans.

NB. This upstairs venue is now open most nights of the week, showcasing local bands and other events.

For the Zodiac and Bullingdon Arms see club reviews.

MUSICAL INSTRUMENT SHOPS

The Music Room

27 Park End Street (01865) 249292
www.the-music-room.com Open 9.30am-5pm

An impressive collection of acoustic 'folk' instruments, ranging from banjos, fiddles, mandolins, and bouzoukis to accordions. While you're here, expect a good natter about the folk scene with owner, Bill, and, if you're lucky, he might even share his enthusiasm for real ale and narrow boats with you, too.

Also stocking tutor books and CDs, the cheapest things you'll find here are Morris bells for 26p, while their most impressive instruments are their range of handmade 'Heartwood' guitars, which

VENUES

Brookes University

Top of Headington Hill

With a capacity of around 1000 this is the place to come and see the big boys play. In recent years it has also been a popular venue for the occasional 'secret', warm-up gigs from the likes of Blur and Ash. It's a bit of a trek up the hill if you're coming from town, but the thought of being so close to those pale, scrawny, young, Indie gods should spur you on.

Spin (Upstairs at the Wheatsheaf)

129 High Street (01865) 721156 Thursdays

From sozzled old Jazz legends to inebriated old Blues heroes, the list of bands and musicians who have played upstairs at the Wheatsheaf is an impressive one. In fact, Spin has been attracting a wide age-range of faithful music-lovers for umpteen years now, and, owing to the fact that most other venues in Oxford have since closed or been turned into lap-dancing clubs, this is probably now one of Oxford's oldest and a must for all music fans seeking refuge from DJ culture. A word of advice though - it definitely pays to get here early, as seating is limited, and getting stuck at the back by the bar

Bert Jansch took a fancy to recently. Friendly and well informed, if you're looking for a quality traditional instrument, there's nowhere in Oxford better.

Music Box
Cowley Road (01865) 204119

Run by the ex-singer of Go West, this tiny, second-hand music shop at the bottom end of Cowley Road is crammed with everything from guitars and amps to second-hand sitars, mandolins, and even an original boxed Rolf Harris Stylophone. The guys in here seem up for a haggle, so, if you share a fag with them and tell them how much you loved 'We close our eyes', they'll probably do you a good discount. Also, a good place to look for band members, as the door is always littered with ads.

ENGLAND
Squeaky frog used as a toy. The frog contains a small free reed which squeaks when it is pressed.
d.d. H. La Rue, 1986.

Professional Music Technology
Cowley Road (01865) 725221

The best selection of guitars, amps, drums, effects and computer technology in Oxford (although the competition is hardly fierce).

They also seem to specialise in Peavey and Marshall amps and will do a good part-exchange deal for your crappy old original Vox AC 30.

Most likely to say:
'Oh it's great little piece of equipment that is, the guys from Radiohead bought a couple of those last week mate.'

Least likely to say:
'The bloke over the road from Go West used to own that keyboard'.

Oxford in books & the Movies

OXFORD IN THE MOVIES

Accident
Dir. Jospeh Losey 1967

Dirk Bogarde plays a fellow of Magdalen College obsessed with one of his female students and, as the theme of infidelity slowly becomes apparent, it moves through the lives of the people around him, gradually pulling them apart. With a tense script from Harold Pinter, the film is pieced together with his trademark stilted conversations and pregnant pauses and, as the rot sets in, the characters try to remain terribly English about it all within their (ironically) civilised University surroundings. Highly recommended.

Laurel and Hardy's 'A Chump at Oxford'
Dir. Alfred Goulding 1939

Inadvertently having foiled a bank robbery, the hapless duo is rewarded with a chance to gain a proper education at Oxford. On their arrival, the students take every opportunity to lampoon them until Stan receives a blow on the head, which reveals him to be an English aristocrat who had been suffering amnesia. The scene in Oxford maze should be enough to make anyone even vaguely familiar with the city realise that it was all filmed in the studio, but it's still an endearing classic from The Laurel and Hardy vaults, with plenty of clichéd English catchphrases like 'Well done, old bean' and 'He's jolly well asking for a punch on the nose.' Look out for a cameo from the very young master of horror, Peter Cushing.

The Madness of King George
Dir. Nicholas Hytner 1994

Nigel Hawthorne plays the king with the unruly stools in this moving and occasionally funny historical drama about George III. The film was shot close to Oxford and the Bodleian Library was used for the House of Commons scenes.

Oxford Blues
Dir. Robert Boris 1984

Rob Lowe plays a tiresome and obnoxious American who wangles his way to the University. Once there he is properly 'educated' by fellow students in the arts of rowing and saying 'okay ya' and, consequently, woos a rich young lady. Insulting, boring and with surprisingly few shots of Rob Lowe in the nude. Retitled by Time Out as 'A wank in Oxford'.

175

Shadowlands
Dir. Richard Attenborough 1993

Set in Oxford in the 1950s, this is the slow, atmospheric tale of CS Lewis (played by Anthony Hopkins) and the surprising but tragic love affair he had late in life with an American admirer, Joy Gresham. There are plenty of scenes of Magdalen College and the Cloisters, as well as scenes of May morning and even Lewis and his writers' group, The Inklings, down the Eagle and Child (except it isn't really). Quite a simple, uncluttered film for Attenborough, with Hopkins sympathetically playing Lewis as a man who learns to simultaneously suffer and love, by liberating himself from the sheltered life he has built.

Tom and Viv
Dir Brian Gilbert 1994

Nothing to get too excited about in this slow account of TS Eliot and his hormonally imbalanced wife. Early on the film contained brief snippets of Merton College where Elliot studied, then I fell asleep.

Wilde
Dir. Brian Gilbert Year 1997

A rather tepid account of Wilde's ill-fated relationship with Alfred Lord Douglas. Stephen Fry plays a surprisingly placid Oscar Wilde and even the occasional shots of Jude Law's bottom do little to relieve the monotony of it all. Wilde's old college Magdalen gets a brief look in while the scenes of Wilde's imprisonment were filmed in Oxford jail shortly after it was closed.

The Young Sherlock Holmes
Dir. Barry Levinson 1988

Shots of Radcliffe Square and other parts of Oxford come into this tale as a pre-pubescent Holmes and Watson try to discover why an Egyptian loony has been going around killing everyone. Worth seeing just to witness the scene where a malevolent hat-stand comes to life.

OTHERS TO LOOK FOR

Heaven's Gate
Dir. Michael Cimino 1980

Mansfield College was bizarrely transformed into an American campus complete with stick-on leaves for this 19th century Western.

True Blue
Dir. Ferdinand Fairfax 1996

Based around the 1987 boat race, this film has lots of shots of the river, the boathouse and other parts of Oxford, but lets itself down by being desperately dull.

The Harry Potter Films

Both Christ Church's dining hall and staircase have featured in the Harry Potter films, though you'll have to have eagle eyes to spot them through all the computer graphics.

Oxford has always had a rich literary history; something in the region of 500 novels featuring this celebrated city have, to date, been published, although over half of these are by Colin Dexter. The list of famous authors who studied at the colleges is pretty exhaustive too, and includes such giants as Oscar Wilde, Evelyn Waugh, Percy Shelley, T.E. Lawrence, Aldous Huxley, Grahame Greene and W.B. Yeats, while in more recent years the University has educated the likes of Martin Amis, John Fowles, Iris Murdoch, Ian McEwan and Will Self.

To mention all the important Oxford literary figures is a book in itself, but the four local writers perhaps most celebrated for their work (and all, curiously, authors of Fantasy-based fiction that appeals to children and adults alike), are: C.S. Lewis, Lewis Carroll, J.R.R. Tolkien and Philip Pullman.

C.S. Lewis

The author of the Narnia books and Screwtape letters lived and lectured in Oxford for many years up to his death in 1963. Narniaphiles frequently still seek out Lewis's grave at Headington Quarry Trinity church, which also has etchings of Narnia on its windows. In no way cashing in on the Narnia legend, the church also has a selection of tea towels and mugs for sale on the Narnia theme. Over the ring road in Risinghurst, you'll find Lewis Close. At the end on the right is Lewis's house, 'The Kiln', and, beyond there, the nature reserve said to have inspired the Narnia chronicles, as well as Tolkien's Middle Earth. Follow the path around the stagnant pond up the hill to the right and past the wooden building and you'll get a surprisingly good view of the town. Lewis fans might find it a bit disappointing though, as it really isn't all that magical.

OXFORD IN BOOKS & THE MOVIES

Lewis Carroll and Alice in Wonderland

Lewis Carroll was the pen-name of Charles Dodgeson, a mathematics lecturer at Christ Church, who, in the late 19th century, enjoyed spending time with Alice Liddell, daughter of the then Dean of the college.

Legend has it the tale originated came about from a boat trip up the River Godstow where Dodgeson took Alice and her sister one summer. The girls begged Dodgeson for a story and so he spun the ever-more fantastical tale of the adventures Alice might get up to in another world.

It is believed that Dodgeson's relationship with Alice may not have been entirely innocent, and the fact that he kept a darkroom in his lodgings and liked to take photos of naked children does nothing to disprove these allegations. In fact, Oxford author David Horan went as far as to call him *'an emotionally retarded pervert from whom any sensible parents would today keep their children well away.'*

Fans of the book can find a gift shop opposite Christ Church where you can buy everything from Alice postcards to Alice anti-dandruff shampoo. This shop used to be Alice's favourite sweet shop, which Dodgeson re-named the Old Sheep Shop in Alice Through the Looking Glass.

For a modern-day version of Alice in Wonderland, read Automated Alice by Jeff Noon, where Alice falls into a computer terminal and ends up in an alternative Manchester – it's a wonderful twist on the original.

J.R.R. Tolkien

John Ronald Reuel Tolkien was a professor at Merton College, and a specialist in Old and Middle English when he first came up with the idea for the Hobbit. Basing much of the character of Bilbo on himself (a conservative, pipe-smoking, nature-lover who hated travelling and mechanisation and had very hairy feet), Tolkien set out to write the kind of mythological epic that he believed was 'sorely lacking' in English society. The Hobbit was a huge success, and, though disappointment followed with his next work, the Silmarillion, Tolkien was encouraged by his writers' group 'The Inklings' and former student W.H. Auden to write a sequel to The Hobbit. Drawing on his childhood and experiences of fighting the Great War, Tolkien wrote his masterpiece, the Lord of the Rings, which took him sixteen years to complete. The book achieved cult success, particularly with the burgeoning Hippy Scene of the Sixties who adopted such slogans as: 'Gandalph for President', 'Tolkien is Hobbit-forming' and ' Saruman is a bastard'.

Tolkien, sadly, did not relish the fame his books brought him, and particularly did not enjoy being constantly phoned up at three a.m. by Californian Hippy Space Cadets asking to speak to Frodo. He changed address, went ex-directory and finally moved to Bournemouth. After the death of his wife, Edith, in 1971, Tolkien moved back to Oxford

J.R.R. TOLKIEN WITH THE INKLINGS

and took rooms at his former college, where he died on September 2nd 1973. His grave lies in Wovercote Cemetery, north of the ring road.

Lord of the Rings was subsequently voted 'Book of the Century' in 1998, and since the success of the three blockbuster movies that came out in the early Noughties, it appears that sales of his books have reached a scale Tolkien could never have imagined in his lifetime. Despite the cynical, post-modern times we live in, it seems that Tolkien's complex but naive fantasy world still remains 'Hobbit Forming'.

For more info, visit www.tolkiensociety.org

Penguin Modern Classics

Max Beerbohm
Zuleika Dobson

The sparkling, wicked and delicious story
of a *femme fatale*

RECOMMENDED READING

Zuleika Dobson
(Max Beerbohm)

Like his friend and confidant, Oscar Wilde, Max only ever wrote one novel in his lifetime but, as with Wilde, his work possesses a wit and intelligence rarely found in other writers.

Beerbohm's novel, ironically subtitled 'an Oxford Love Story', describes the tale of the beautiful but vacuous Miss Dobson who, upon her arrival in Oxford, drives all of its students to distraction. The vain Miss Dobson, applying the Grouch Marx adage of not wanting to belong to any club that would have her as a member, takes no interest in the men around her until she is snubbed by the noble and handsome Duke Of Dorset. Naturally, Zuleika falls madly in love with him, believing she has finally found a worthy suitor. Alas, upon discovering that the Duke *reciprocates* her love Zuleika cruelly casts him aside. In a fit of pique the Duke stupidly declares that he will drown himself in the Isis, whereupon all the other students decide to follow suit.

Not just a parody of romantic fiction, with Zuleika Dobson Beerbohm created an extremely original black comedy that subtly lampoons the traditions of the upper classes, the University and the students themselves. The book is also peppered with ethereal characters, from Greek gods and ghosts to the 'talking' heads on the Sheldonian, while Beerbhom's prose is sardonic, surreal and extremely playful; he even shows up himself a couple of times in the novel, once to justify his 'expertise' in telling such a tale, and at another point, to lambaste the reader for daring to question his actions.

This truly is a forgotten masterpiece of early twentieth century comic literature, and, though it is, I fear, out of print, Beerbohm's novel can be picked up fairly easily in some of the second-hand bookshops in the city.

Oxford by David Horan
(from the cities of the imagination series)

Eloquently written and packed with wonderful stories and interesting facts, this book outshines all others on the shelves if you want to learn more about the city. Not strictly a guide, the book instead takes the reader on a slow sprawling journey across the city whilst moving forward through history. While all other books about Oxford seem to linger far too long on rather tedious architectural facts and dates about colleges, Horan knows that the secret is in the telling of the tale.

Strange Oxford
(Oxford Golden Dawn Publishing)

Discover the Oxford of pagan wells, giants, ley-lines and witches. This wonderful DIY booklet takes the reader to some relatively unexplored corners of the town, as well as places to visit in Oxfordshire, from stone circles to chalk figures on hillsides. Some of Oxford's more mystical figures are celebrated too, including Yeats, the Hellfire Club, and one-time demonologist Montague Summers, who, legend has it, was turned into a giraffe by Aleister Crowley, *'though Summers did not appear to notice.'* (Best place to find this is the Inner Bookshop or, failing that, call Golden Dawn Publishing)

PHILIP PULLMAN*

Branded 'the most dangerous man in Britain', Philip Pullman is one of the most exciting, intelligent and uncompromising novelists working today. He has bagged a clutch of literary prizes and accolades from every quarter, yet attracted much adverse press, and a grilling courtesy of the South Bank Show. He enjoys a wide readership and distinguished figures, such as Sir Tom Stoppard and Sam Mendes, lining up to adapt his works, yet has also prompted outrage in some parts of America and the condemnation of the Pope. What is more remarkable is that the centre of all this controversy is, ostensibly, 'only a children's writer', with a self-confessed fondness for fairy tales.

Pullman, a one-time Oxford English teacher and Exeter College scholar, had been writing for nearly twelve years, producing a series of excellent kids' books that won praise, but little else. 'His Dark Materials', his best-selling trilogy, changed all that. By the time the last volume, 'The Amber Spyglass', hit the shelves, it had become the publishing event of the decade, and was the first children's novel to win the Whitbread Prize. J.K. Rowling may have sold more, but plaudits of the kind heaped on Pullman have, so far, eluded her.

Unsurprisingly for an Oxford writer, the trilogy is a sprawling fantasy. Indeed, it owes rather a lot to its eminent Oxford forebears, the Tolkien and Lewis sagas, and takes, like the latter, Milton's 'Paradise Lost' as a starting point. (The title is a quotation from Book One of the epic poem). There, however, all similarity ends; while the 'Narnia' tales are thinly veiled Christian parables, Pullman's story of Lyra and Will, two children from different universes joining forces in a plot to assassinate God, is quite clearly an outright attack on the Church. (My God! Think of the children!)

Equally unsurprisingly, Oxford figures largely in the work. Twice. Will's Oxford is the one we know and love; Lyra's is subtly different. All the recognizable elements are there, but re-arranged somehow, rather as in Hardy's 'Christminster' (see "Jude The Obscure"). Many towns in parallel universes feature in the trilogy, but it is to our Oxford, for obvious reasons, that Pullman fans make their pilgrimage, (although trips to Cittagazze are available through Cheeky from Spring 2004). You can make a tour of the places and objects that appear in the book: the most popular attractions being the trepanned skull in the Pitt Rivers, and the bench, in the Botanical Gardens, where Will and Lyra spend their last hour together. Here, fans of a sentimental bent have even been known to leave flowers and tokens in honour of the (very) young lovers.

If all this seems confusing, read the books. 'His Dark Materials' is one of those works that seem immeasurably diminished by any attempts at summary. This man really knows how to tell a story. The greatest favour I could do you would be to sit you down, thrust a copy of 'Northern Lights', the first part, in your hands, and stand over you until you've read it cover to cover. You might think I'm a dangerous madman, but you'll thank me for it when you're begging for the next instalment.

Pullman's earlier books have enjoyed greater sales recently on the back of the trilogy's success, and this is no bad thing. The 'Sally Lockhart' series, concerning a sort of feisty, young, female Sherlock Holmes, is particularly fine, but it is the novella, 'Clockwork', an E.T.A. Hoffmann inspired fairy tale, that perhaps lays the strongest claim on your attention. Complex, funny, terrifying and moving, and written in prose like cool, fresh water, it is worth a dozen 'Booker' winners any day.

* many thanks to our esteemed editor, Brian Mitchell for this piece

Subversive Oxford

Oxford has always been a hotbed of political activity, not just churning out Tory and Labour MPs at the universities but also Green campaigners, Squatters' Rights groups and many others. This is the birthplace of Oxfam, Earthfirst! (an organisation which fuelled countless protests and demonstrations), Corporate Watch and Land is Ours - a land reclamation group run by Guardian columnist and Newsnight favourite, George Monbiot.

Undercurrents

16b Cherwell Street Oxford (01865) 203661
www.undercurrents.org

With umpteen videos, two activists' handbooks, and several awards under their belt, you have to admire the hard work these guys have done. Undercurrent videos are the result of video activists' work from around the world, filming and documenting news that the media would rather we didn't see.

For an alternative tour of Oxford, Undercurrents 5 is a must, with a truly comic scene of Tory transport minister Sir George Young being chased around town by restless natives. Oxford's biggest street party can also be seen on Undercurrents 6, when 'Reclaim the Streets' turned Cowley Road into one big festival.

The Undercurrents website is extremely informative, and a good starting point for anyone interested in getting involved in the local anti-globalisation movement. It's also worth checking to see if they still do screenings at the UPP every couple of months by looking in the local press or any of the shops, like Uhuru, up the Cowley Road.

The latest offerings from Undercurrents include a series of new video CDROMs covering such topics as Globalisation, and featuring the likes of Noam Chomsky.

Subverts

If you ever wondered who is responsible for defacing the billboards around town, then you have this bunch to thank. Aiming to put a little more honesty into some of the sugary sloganeering of multinationals and crappy car companies, their graffiti can be seen in the Cowley triangle or anywhere a McDonald's advert is to be found skulking. Again, if you want to get involved, your first port of call should probably be the guys at Undercurrents.

Oxford's most celebrated subversive: Howard Marks

Once the world's most-wanted man, Marks was, for twenty-five years, the biggest dope-smuggler in the world. This Balliol graduate took a puff of a joint in the 60s and found his vocation in life. Immortalised in the Super Furry Animals song 'Hanging out with Howard Marks', his more recent exploits include setting up the Cannabis Party (you can guess their policies) and endlessly touring and then scrounging joints from the audience.

I once saw Marks performing in Brighton when, during the questions and answers at the end, someone asked –
Did you ever know Bill Clinton while you were in Oxford?
Marks replied with a twinkle in his eye –
*'Yeah, I met him on several occasions. And I happen to know that he **did** inhale, and plenty more besides. I should know – I sold him the stuff.'*

STRANGE SOCIETIES

Oxford seems to have more than its fair share of neo-hippies, pagans, UFOlogists, and occultists, so if Aleister Crowley, Mulder and Scully, or Tom Baker are your Gods, this might be a good place to start looking.

The UFO Society / Contact Awareness

Contact Michael Soper
(01865) 726908
Box 23 Wheatley

Set up in 1969 by Lord Something-or-other, Contact Awareness has grown to become one of the main archivists of UFO sightings, with over 80,000 now under its belt. It organises public meetings, sky-watches and debates, as well as producing four magazines a year for all you budding X-Filers. To join costs a trifling £9 a year and, as organiser Michael Soper told me, *'It might attract the odd weirdo, but you can guarantee that at least they'll be interesting weirdos'.*

NB. In recent years the Oxford Centre for Crop Circle Studies merged with Contact Awareness, so the group now include this phenomenon too in their on-going research.

Oxfordshire Pagan Circle

PO Box 250 Oxford OX1 1AP
Tel Mog (01865) 243671
mandrake@mandrake.uk.net

Describing Paganism as 'an exploration of Earth and its sites,' the Pagan circle is a melting pot for Pagans of all shapes and sizes to meet and share their ideas. The group also organise regular events around the festival days of the solstices, the equinoxes, Beltane and Halloween, as well as just enjoying a pint and a natter down the pub.

For those into the more serious practice of ritual magic, Oxford's Golden Dawn Occult Society (of which W.B. Yeats was once a member) can be contacted through the same address, as can Golden Dawn Publishing Company who publish books on occultism and witchcraft. For a fact-sheet send a SAE to the above address.

Sex & Fetish

Despite the reputation of a certain club night at the Zodiac, Oxford students do **not** spend all their time rutting like rabbits. In fact a recent survey on the sexual antics of students in the UK revealed Oxford to be the 'least-sexed University in the country,' suggesting that the scholars here are usually far too busy writing essays or reading Proust to ever contemplate an evening of fellatio with a friend. And, for a place its size, Oxford really does have very little to offer in the way of merchandise for the sexually liberated or simply curious. Despite this, there are a few places you can seek out, should you wish to spice up your sex life, or merely to fantasise about having one.

Private Shop

54 Cowley Road (01865) 246958
Open 9.30am-8pm Mon-Sat

Considerably friendlier and less seedy than its neighbour below, this is kind of a hardcore Ann Summers as, along with videos and mags (including back-issues of the imaginatively titled 'Huge Tits'), it stocks dildos, inflatable women, novelty sex toys and a few items of 'sexy' clothing.

Private Lines

Cowley Road (next to Polar Bear)

Spectacularly tacky, squalid and with stupidly over-priced stock (their range of dildos are inferior versions of ones that can be found in Ann Summers for a third of the price), this place will probably have closed down by the time this book goes to print. Probably.

EVERYONE'S TALKING ABOUT KINKY BOOTS...

If it's fantasy bedroom-wear you're after, forget it, you came to the wrong town, but shoe/ boot fetishists may be heartened to know that Fitrite on the High Street sell a small selection of fetish boots, Kitten Heels, and the odd kinky nurse's outfit.

Adult Bookshop
86 Cowley Road (01865) 798287

If you can deal with stepping into this Sixties Soho time-warp, you'll find a wide range of porn videos for £40, DVDs for £30 and a vast array of Jazz Mags, for about a tenner each. There's a pretty good selection of bondage and SM for the pervs, a modest range of gay and TV and all the usual stuff like Young Snatch, Rump and Readers' Wives.

Borders
At the far end of the ground floor, those liberated Americans stock an excellent selection of erotic literature, sex guides, photo-collections, and sexy coffee table books* from the likes of Taschen.

*By that I don't mean books with pictures of sexy coffee tables

SEX & FETISH

The Oxford Gay Scene

Oxford has a small but well-established gay scene, accepted by an open-minded population here and kept fresh by a steady influx of new students. While the Northgate Hall in the town centre is its HQ, the gay community itself is spread thinly around Jericho and East Oxford. The Cowley Road area is a popular hang out, judging by how the crowds at the Bully and Zodiac seem relaxed about the rampant snogging sessions I've witnessed there on several occasions. To avoid trouble, loitering around George Street and Park End Street at night is not the best idea, although this advice applies to all who shy away from the company of pissed-up morons.

While cruising seems mainly confined to the established gay bars and clubs, lovers of the great outdoors might find that Angel Meadow (by Magdalen Bridge) has a reputation as a good meeting spot. But if, at the end of the day, you still need something more exotic, remember London is only a bus-ride away, or you could always buy a copy of the Cheeky Guide to Brighton and spend a dirty weekend there instead.

The Northgate Hall

(Oxford's Lesbian and Gay Community Centre)
St Michael's St (01865) 200249
Members Only (£12 annual membership)

Oxford's gay and lesbian community centre has been on the go for over ten years now, offering women-only and mixed nights every weekend. And, after a recent fire, has even had a much-needed face-lift.

Your initial reaction on walking into one of the evenings here will probably be – *'oh my god, I've walked into a village hall.'* And while, unfortunately, resembling a soiree put on by the local vicar, the nights here are well-loved social events and, if you're gay and new to Oxford, you'll find a welcoming and friendly crowd here.

The Castle

24 Paradise Street (01865) 201510

Oxford's newest gay pub offers Karaoke (downstairs in the Rainbow Room), bar snacks, the latest queer papers, and those obligatory free condoms.

The Jolly Farmer

Paradise Street (01865) 793759

Oxford's first gay pub, the Jolly Farmer leans clearly towards an established older gay male crowd, but is very welcoming to new faces. It's also got a beer garden and a reputation for good food at lunchtime.

Loveshack at the Coven 2
Every Friday since 1856 A.D.
Oxpens Road (01865) 242770

The Coven is one of those tacky Eighties clubs modelled on the cave from the Sixties TV series Batman, but with two floors instead of one, and a distinct lack of men in satin capes poring over ticker-tape in the corner.

Loveshack itself is an evening of tight t-shirts, kitsch music and flashing lights, with the intimate upstairs part of the club turning into a kind of sing-a-long disco area while the downstairs is reserved for banging House. Although popular with lesbians, the night is very male dominated, and the ladies toilets seem a particularly popular haunt for camp conversations, and other leisure activities.

This is without doubt the best place for cruising in Oxford and for men there's everything on offer here: from the lean mean machines wandering around showing off their muscles, to the older beer-swigging types, with shirts hanging over their jeans to hide their pot-bellies.

STUDENTS

The LGB society is a good place to make friends and connections, especially if you're coming out. They also have a drinks night every Thursday in a different college bar, although, whenever it's the turn of Oriel, everyone seems to be washing their hair that night.

ACCOMMODATION

Try the following below for gay accommodation, but don't be surprised if most of the ads turn out to be along the lines of –
'Lesbian non-smoking cat-lover seeks someone to share allotment.'
This **is** oxford after all.

Uhuru
Cowley Road 48 Cowely Road (01865) 248249

Magic Cafe
110 Magdalen Road (01865) 794604

Contact Numbers / Websites

Gay Oxford
PO Box 144 (01865) 251402 Organises talks, walks and other events.

Lesbian, Gay & Bisexual line
(01865) 726893

Wayout Lesbian & Gay Youth Group
(01865) 243389

Oxford Lesbian & Gay Centre
Northgate Hall St Michael's St (01865) 200249

Lesbian, Gay & Bisexual Handbook for Students
available from OUSU

Queer rights committee
(01865) 270777

www.queeroxford.co.uk
This website offers daily information, useful contact numbers, sport information, and competitions (invariably asking the viewer to identify the names of minor characters from Seventies musicals)..

Mind Body Spirit

With everything from floatation tanks to Buddhist temples, and more acupuncturists per square foot than anywhere else in the UK, if you're looking for spiritual nourishment, Oxford's got the lot.

SHOPPING

Culpepper

7 New Inn Hall St (01865) 249754
Open 9am-5.50pm Mon-Sat

Herbs, cosmetics, aromatherapy oils, candles etc.

The Inner Bookshop

(see review in bookshops)

Neal's Yard Remedies

The High and 5 Golden Walk Cross,
Cornmarket Street (01865) 245436
Open 9am-6pm daily 11am-4pm Sun

Comprehensive stock of essential oils, herbs, vitamins, homeopathic remedies and self-help books. The staff will give advice on any common illnesses and can recommend practitioners for anything more serious.

ORGANIC / GM FREE & HEALTH FOOD

Alcock's Butchers

273A Banbury Road Summertown
(01865) 515658

Additive-free meat, organic dairy, fruit, and veg.

Uhuru

48 Cowley Road (01865) 248249

Wholefood, organic produce, non-dairy produce, gluten-free, yeast-free, cruelty-free, born free, I'm free…(sorry, got a bit carried away there)…and body products. Their organic apple pies, organic mint chocolate and homemade flapjack come recommended.

Gibbons Bakery

16 Hertford Street, just off Magdalen Road
(01865) 241136

Don't let the name put you off, you won't be finding black hairs in your baps. Mr Gibbons has been working here for 40 years now, so you could say he's a man that knows his bread.

As well as being one of the few places in Oxford to sell fresh organic bread, they also do the very marvellous Cotswold Crunch.

For organic and vegetarian restaurants see 'Food'

CLINICS & DROP IN CENTRES

Eau De Vie Floatation Centre

34 Cowley Road (01865) 200678
www.eaudevie.net
Open 10am-9.30pm Mon-Fri,
10am-7.30pm Sat £30 for a one- hour floatation, 10% student discount available
Also offering a range of complementary medicines from full-body massage and aromatherapy to reflexology
Floatation and massage together: £55

Going in a floatation tank is one of those experiences everyone should try. You climb into what looks like a skip, gentle music plays for 10 minutes, and then you're left floating in the dark in Epsom salts, feeling like Major Tom. All senses are cut-off, feeling and seeing nothing as you lie there (earplugs and butt-plugs are available for serious floaters). Apparently, 90% of brain activity revolves around stopping us falling over under the influence of gravity, so floatation is something of a night off for this over-burdened organ. Go on, treat your brain to a holiday.

The WellBeing Clinic

30-32 Westminster Way 0845 330 3930
Probably the most comprehensive collection of complimentary medicines in Oxford, with everything from acupuncture and homoeopathy to Alexander Technique, massage and more. Some therapists will do cheap rates for low wage earners.

Focus 4 Health

235 Cowley Road (01865) 790235
Open 9am-6pm Mon-Fri
10% discount for students

Another popular clinic for complementary medicines, ranging from osteopathy to aromatherapy. They've also got rooms you can rent should you need to give a live demonstration of colonic irrigation.

The Notice Boards at the Inner Bookshop and Magic Café

Magdalen Road

These are always crammed with adverts for healers, therapists, Pagan groups, music events and other stuff. Plus, if you're after something yourself, you can stick up your own ad.

WHERE TO FIND OUT MORE

Green Pages £3

You'll find copies of this publication in places like the Tourist Information Centre and in shops up the Cowley Road. It details everything from complementary medicine, counselling, conservation groups, veggie shops and yoga classes.

Madame Colonic

What's On

DIARY OF EVENTS

Torpids and Eights
Wednesday to Saturday first week in March and June (01865) 790268

Inter-collegiate boat races held on the river Isis to sort out the mice from the men. In summer the turnout is impressive, with particularly large crowds turning up on the Saturday for the event held between Donnington Bridge and The Head of the River pub. Bring a picnic and join the throngs for an afternoon's 'bumping'.

Turn up on the last day and you may even witness the wonderful tradition of the cox (the one who sits at the top of the boat and hurls abuse at the crew for not rowing hard enough) being thrown in the water and drowned.

Poohsticks World Championship
(01491) 838294 david@dcaswell.f9.co.uk
End of March Starts noon at Days Lock
Little Wittenham www.pooh-sticks.com

Come and join grown men and women from all over the globe in throwing twigs off a bridge for the coveted title of 'Poohsticks World Champion'. There are competitions for individuals and teams (the Welsh are a pretty formidable team apparently), and you can even bring along your favourite Teddy bear, as an expert 'teddyatrician' will be on hand to give advice as to age, value and any necessary surgery. Remember, this is for charity, so no cheating please; the contestant who brought a motorised stick last year was dealt with very severely. Contact the number / email above for more details on how to enter.

Oxford v Cambridge University Boat Race

Usually takes place at the weekend in late March/ early April For more information call Iffley Road Sport's Centre (01865) 240476 *www.theboatrace.org*

This famous race happens not in Oxford but along a four and a half mile stretch between Putney and Mortlake in London and is regularly watched by up to 250,000 spectators along the banks of the River Thames. Overall, Cambridge is currently in the lead with something like 77 wins to Oxford's 69, but they also hold the record for sinking the most, at four sinks to Oxford's measly two (although in 1912 both teams somehow managed to sink simultaneously).

Zippo's Circus

Twice a year (Usually Tues-Sun, middle of March and October/ November) Call Tourist Information (01865) 726871 for more details

Hosted every year by Papa Lazaru and the gang, this is a cruelty-free non-animal circus, whose acrobatics and other mischief usually take place in the grounds of either the Ice Rink or South Parks.

Hard-Boiled Egg Race

End of April bank holiday Monday 11am-12.30pm Shotover Plain Carpark (01865) 715830 for more details

This fine, 100-year-old tradition takes place every Easter, involving egg-races

and a huge picnic. Bring along some cucumber sandwiches and lashings of ginger beer and, of course, your own lovingly painted hard-boiled egg. There are prizes for the best-painted egg followed by the Demolition Derby. The egg that rolls the fastest and furthest down the hill is the winner, but watch out for monsters (in the guise of cardboard boxes with cut-out mouths) who will eat your egg given half the chance. One year some joker put an explosive in his monster, which blew up the first egg that went in. Be in the car park by 11am with your hard-boiled egg and get ready for what must be the event of the year.

May Morning

May 1st 6am Magdalen Bridge and the rest of town

One of the more important and exciting days in Oxford's calendar. This tradition, to most ignoramuses, simply means that the pubs magically open at 6am, but May morning is, in fact, an ancient spring celebration with its roots firmly embedded in Pagan ritual.

Set your alarm for 5am, drag yourself out of bed and make your way to Magdalen Bridge to witness the college choristers sing carols and madrigals from the top of Magdalen tower. The whole of the High Street is usually mobbed for this and it is quite a spectacle. For centuries students have also followed an age-old custom of jumping off the bridge into the river, but in the last few years the police have stopped it on the grounds that it was 'silly' and that 'someone might get hurt', which is of course the whole point.

After the choir have finished with a rousing version of 'Morning has Broken', the bells are rung to greet the new spring and around the town you'll see Morris dancers prancing gaily. Some of the more serious Pagan worshippers even come out wearing giant phalluses, as this was, traditionally, a time for celebrating fertility, but if you've ever seen The Wickerman' you'll know it's best to keep well out of their way.

Having experienced all this, you'll then want to tuck yourself up in a warm, busy pub and experience the peculiar feeling of getting drunk first thing in the morning. Chances are, by mid-morning you'll want to go back to bed, but your friends will egg you on to have another couple of pints ensuring that the rest of the day will be just a haze. But don't worry, the whole town is usually one mass hangover by mid-afternoon.

Mayday fact number 1: Walloping

As mentioned above, May Day in Oxford has its roots in Pagan folklore. In the 1600s it wouldn't be uncommon to see college Dons, wearing enormous multi-coloured strap-on phalluses, parading through the streets in search of unwary students. Custom decreed that, if caught, the student would have to submit to what was known as a 'walloping ' from the brightly coloured phallus. Then both student and tutor would engage in a merry little dance, involving buttock slapping and gargling the national anthem, and the two would finally slip off somewhere discreet to swap phone numbers.

Of course, this practice has fallen by the wayside now, but some college tutors are still anxious to keep it alive, particularly those from St John's and Christchurch.

MayDay fact number 2: The Choir

It is a closely-guarded secret that a live choir has not sung from Magdalen Tower on May morning for over 30 years now, and that all the madrigals, hymns and Soft Rock ballads heard by the dawn crowds are actually played on Magdalen College's state-of-the-art Amstrad tape-deck. Listen carefully after the choristers sing 'American Pie' and you can actually hear the tape being turned over.

Controversy reigned in 1974 when, during a sombre madrigal, someone accidentally knocked the switch on the machine to 'tuner', and the crowds were subjected to 90 seconds of local news, weather and an advert for the Assam Balti.

Mayfly
May bank-holiday Monday, South Parks
(01865) 467259
www.visitoxford.org

Huge crowds regularly turn up for this family event held in South Park just off St Clement's. Expect local bands, a radio road-show, clowns, fire-eaters, jugglers, bouncy castles and a fun fair.

Balloon Fiesta
Usually held the second weekend in May, Cutteslowe Park Admission £2
This weekend jamboree has, in the past, involved such attractions as bike stunts, dog display teams and majorettes, but don't worry – there's some good stuff as well. On Saturday evening a load of hot air balloons are launched high up into the night sky for an event known as 'Nightglow' where the balloons line up and burn torches to the accompaniment of Chris de Burgh's 'Lady in Red'. This is followed by a well-deserved fireworks display.

Lord Mayor's Parade
Bank holiday Monday end of May
(01865) 467259

Starting at St Giles and finishing at South Parks, this colourful procession of floats and live Folk music is Oxford's answer to the Mardi Gras.

Early May Eights Week
(see earlier listings)

Beating the bounds
(Ascension Day)
29th May Church of St Michael at the Northgate 9am

Come and watch loonies wander around the city hitting it with sticks. A must for Monty Python fans. For more details see 'A-Z of Traditions and Terminology'.

Encaenia
12pm Ninth week of Trinity Term on Wednesday in June

This annual tradition is when all the college officials parade through town in their Sunday best to the Sheldonian Theatre where they bestow honorary degrees on the famous and wealthy.

Jazz in the Park
South Park, first Sunday in August Free
(01865) 467259

Witness South Park transform into a sea of corduroy, goatee beards and caps. Nice.

St Giles' Fair
Held Monday and Tuesday in September after the first Sunday unless the Sunday is the first. (If you read it again it'll make sense)
For hundreds of years now St Giles has welcomed this two-day fair which brings a wonderful chaos to the town centre. It is certainly more for the Town than Gown, as the students are

still officially on holiday at this time (although a few do sneak back early to do some girly swatting).

Expect everything from the old carousel-style fairground rides to the modern ones that scare the willies out of me. Plus there are festival stalls with candyfloss, fortune-tellers and all the other usual gubbins. Look out for the tattooed lady; she was, by all accounts, once a promising undergraduate from St Johns, but just couldn't resist the lure of the bright lights and men with lamb-chops and greasy hair.

Lord Mayor's Christmas Carols

Mid-December
Held in the Town Hall (01865) 252838

Christmas wouldn't be Christmas without a hearty rendition of a few Carols. The perfect way to get into the Yuletide spirit, without raiding the drinks' cabinet.

LOCAL WEBSITES & TOURIST INFO

Tourist Information Centre

15 Broad Street (01865) 726871
Open Mon-Sat 9.30am-5pm,
Sun 10am-3.30pm (Easter-late September)

Your one-stop destination for booking hotels, tours, bus trips and finding out what's on, in and around the city. Sure, much of the information here covers the more mainstream aspects of the city's entertainment and you probably won't find out who's playing down the Zodiac tonight, but then you might never have discovered that the Chuckle Brothers were in town if you hadn't popped in.

www.dailyinfo.co.uk

To be honest, if you had a palm pilot you'd be better off throwing this book in the bin and logging on to Dailyinfo. As well as up to the minute information on what's on around Oxford, their website features everything from rooms to let and jobs on offer to webcam views of the city and virtual tours. With over 3,000 hits per day, local news and a 'Notes and Queries' style 'get help for anything' section, it really is, by far, the best Oxford website.

Look out also for their daily posters, found in every college, Brookes University, Tourist Information and Blackwells.

Alternatively you could try:

www.whatsoninoxford.com
www.oxfordinformation.co.uk
www.visitoxford.org

Where to Sleep

Whether you're seeking 16th century cottages with flowery duvets, exotic palatial boudoirs or a rickety sofa bed in someone's garage shed, Oxford has a wide range of accommodation, from the most hardened traveller to the comfort seekers with more money than sense.

While there are many hotels and guest houses scattered all over the town, the majority of these lie on Iffley Road and Banbury Road, and appear to be run by an army of old women who:

- *Have been cloned by the city council.*
- *Are all called Betty.*
- *Will try and sell you their home-made jam and moan about how everyone seemed happier during the war.*

It is worth noting that during the summer months it can become very difficult to get weekend rooms here without booking well in advance, and if you just show up in June during Henley Regatta or Garsington Opera, hoping for the best, you might do well to bring a sleeping bag.

HOTELS

EXPENSIVE
The Old Bank

92-94 High Street, Oxford OX1 4BN
(01865) 799599
info@oldbank-hotel.co.uk

If not the best hotel in Oxford, then certainly the most urbane. Avoiding all that fake Olde English nonsense, that you have to endure in most places here, the Old Bank have, instead, gone for a modern, stylish layout, and every room comes with a large screen TV, full Internet connection and your own CD player, with an assortment of very lame music (unless Kenny G is your idea of sonic craftsmanship). The rooms are, of course, spotless, the staff excellent, and your only reasonable objection could be the price.

This hotel is also occupied by a ghost that lives in the old part of the hotel (from the days when it was Barclay's Bank), and the staff tell grisly tales of the nocturnal spectre drifting into guests' rooms at the stroke of midnight, trying to sell them house insurance.

The cheapest single occupancy is £140, standard doubles start at £160, super-duper double for £200, and the super-super-duper-duper for £235. Suites start at £265 and all fees include VAT (though breakfast is extra).

The Old Parsonage

1 Banbury Road, Oxford OX2 6NN
(01865) 310210
info@oldparsonage-hotel.co.uk

Located very close to town, and with a reputation for being among the finest hotels here, the Old Parsonage is straight out of a Helena Bonham-Carter costume drama, with all the rooms lovingly restored to their original 17th Century design. The antique furniture and abundance of flowery patterns everywhere won't be to everyone's liking, but will probably make American tourists go weak at the knees.

The hotel has a colourful history, with famous guests ranging from Michael Caine to Oscar Wilde who, after returning home late from a heavy Uzo session in Greece, was kicked out of his room at Magdalen College and forced to take up residence here.

Singles £124, doubles £153, suites £193 for double occupancy and £164 for single occupancy. Prices are inclusive of VAT, but, as above, breakfast is extra.

The Randolph

Beaumont Street, Oxford, OX1 2LN
(0870) 400 8200
www.mcdonaldhotels.co.uk

The Randolph is considered, by many, to be the élite hotel in Oxford, and seems to be the favourite destination of the rich and famous. Val Kilmer stayed here for the filming of The Saint (and booked in under the name Simon Templar), the film 'Shadowlands', with Anthony Hopkins, was shot here (although **he** opted to stay at the backpacker hostel), and Tony Blair used to drink here whilst at university.

Despite all its fame and fortune the Randolph is, undoubtedly, very good, but its reputation far exceeds its quality. They've even got one of those horrible teddy bears in a graduation outfit sat in the hallway. Eurgh!

Singles £175, doubles £195 and deluxe suites a snip at £355.

The Eastgate Hotel
Merton Street Oxford OX1 4BE
(0870) 4008201
eastgate@macdonald-hotels.co.uk

Slap, bang, in the middle of town, the Eastgate (part of the Macdonald hotels chain), offers reliable, friendly service, and is just a short walk from the city centre. Prices are steep for the budget traveller, but reasonable compared to other major hotels.

The cheapest single occupancy is £140, doubles start at £160 and there is a 4 poster for £200. Bed and Breakfast bookings are priced at £68 per person, per night based on a double occupancy.

MEDIUM PRICED
Head Of The River
Folly Bridge, Oxford OX1 4LB
(01865) 721600
headoftheriver@fullers.co.uk

Located right on Folly Bridge (with views of the ducks floating by), the rooms in the Head of the River are probably one of Oxford best-kept secrets. Most passers by assume that this is a typical pub from a typical pub chain, but the upstairs offers what may be the best deal for accommodation in the centre of Oxford; twelve spotless, colourful rooms, many with great views and an unbeatable location. *Rooms are affordable, by Oxford standards, with singles at £75, doubles at £85 and family rooms at £95.*

Bath Place Hotel
4-5 Bath Place, Oxford OX1 3SU
(01865) 791812
info@bathplace.co.uk www.bathplace.co.uk

Epitomising the Cheeky Guide philosophy that if you stumble down each and every little passageway beguiling treats can be found, the Bath place hotel is a tiny, but cosy, 17th Century cottage in the very heart of the city centre. If you want a four-poster then take room 11, if you want some colour take room 12, and if you need a little space, try room 9. *The cheapest single occupancy is £90, doubles start at £100 and suites from £125. Breakfast and VAT are included.*

Crazy Bear

Bear Lane, Stadhampton, Oxfordshire
OX44 7UR (01865) 890714
www.crazybearhotel.co.uk
sales@chrazybearhotel.co.uk

Located ten minutes drive out of Oxford, the Crazy Bear is a hotel from heaven. All the rooms are decked out in wild colours, and two of the cottage rooms have entirely stainless steel bathrooms. The Monte Christo Suite here has been voted the sixth most romantic hotel room in the world, and legend has it that Richard Gere first fell in love with a hamster here (?!).

The cottage rooms tend to fill up very fast, so if you are planning on a night of romance in the Monte Christo room, forget spontaneity; it's best to book at least six weeks in advance. *Singles start at £60, doubles at £80. There are five double rooms and two Cottage Rooms, (£140- £160 for the double/ £80-£90 for the single, depending on time of the week).*

Burlington House

374 Banbury Road, Oxford, OX2 7PP
(01865) 513513
www.burlington-house.co.uk
stay@burlington-house.co.uk

This wonderful guesthouse is tastefully decorated (not a flowery pattern to

be found) and is very clean. If travelling alone, try and get the single room in the little Japanese garden, as it is really beautiful. All rooms come with TV, coffee-making facilities etc, but be warned, there is no smoking allowed anywhere within a three miles radius of the hotel, and anyone caught having a crafty fag in the toilet will be nailed up as an example to all other guests. It's a fair old walk to town from here, but, if you're really, nice owner Tony will load you up with jars of homemade granola and biscuits for the journey. As far as medium priced accommodation goes, this couldn't be better.
Singles £38-58, Doubles £80-85.

The Galaxie Hotel

180 Banbury Road, Oxford, OX2 7BT
(O1865) 515688
www.galaxie.co.uk info@galaxie.co.uk

The antithesis of stuffy English hotels, the Galaxie is, instead, lively, fun, colourful and an excellent place to stay, especially in summer.

The layout is very enticing, with a bright breakfast area, sprawling patio and a back garden, which is home to a family of Coi carp and is littered with bonsai trees (which at night attract many of Oxford's pixies community and their dogs).
Singles - £60, Doubles from £88, and, for the cheapskates, there are two extra basic singles, available for £50.

Eurobar

48 George Street, Oxford, OX1 2AQ
(01865) 725087
www.oxfordcity.co.uk/accom/eurobar/

Located pretty close to the train station, and more or less connected to the bus station, the Eurobar is a good place for the weary traveller to stop and rest for the night. This is a young, friendly place with a café to lounge

about in during the day and a cheap and cheerful bar. And while the rooms are not overly exciting, they're certainly very clean. A good place to stay for younger travellers looking for a little more privacy than a hostel.
Singles £45-65, Doubles £59-80

ECONOMY
Brenal Guest House
307 Iffley Road, Oxford,
(01865) 721561

A very agreeable, non-smoking B&B, close to the city centre and offering good meals. The owner gives a great account of one guest who, having returned late to the hotel, found that he had forgotten his keys, so being resourceful decided to procure himself a ladder, and climb up onto the roof and in through his window. This would have been a happy ending if it weren't for the screaming German backpackers, who didn't appreciate him climbing into bed with them.
Singles - £30, doubles - £60. Breakfast included.

Parklands Hotel
100 Banbury Road, Oxford OX2 6JU
(01865) 554374 *stay@parklandsoxford.co.uk*

While there is no Basil, no Polly, no Manuel, no Sybil, no rats and no German guests, this place still, inexplicably, feels like Fawlty Towers. Maybe it's just the layout, I really don't know. The rooms are clean, the menu looks good and it's all generally bright and cheery. Most of the 18 rooms have en suite bathrooms, colour TVs, and tea and coffee makers. Of course you can't see Cowley Beach from here, but the manager suggested maybe we *'take a hotel closer to the sea, or preferably in it.'*
Singles £59, Doubles £89. Breakfast included.

HOSTELS

YHA Youth Hostel
2A Botley Road, Oxford OX2 OAB
(01865) 727275 *oxford@yha.org.uk*

Located right behind the main train station, the YHA Oxford has now cemented its place as the best hostel in Oxford. Normally I avoid the official hostels in favour of the backpacker hostels (the smelly ones where nobody cleans up but the parties are great), but the YHA have done such a great job here, that it cannot be ignored. The place is spotless, fun, extremely well layed out, and offers everything you could want in a hostel, including a private indoor smoking room, video room, library, internet, restaurant, and plenty of places just to laze about in. As far as hostels go, this place is top of the heap.

Dorm rooms are £14pn if you share with 6 people, twin rooms £46. All rooms are en-suite and offer clean linen. Breakfast included.

Oxford Backpackers
9a Hythe Bridge Street, Oxford
(01865) 721761 *www.hostels.co.uk*

As backpacker hostels go, this is pretty standard. There is a pool table, two Internet terminals, some video games, and a good collection of books to keep you occupied. Throughout the building, colourful paintings adorn the walls, while Reggae music plays through the sound systems, and can even be heard in the bathrooms, helping mask the occasional noises of randy young couples. It's not always the cleanest place on the planet, but neither was your room at home before you left to come here.

Owner Dale is a wealth of information on what to do for your stay in Oxford, but unless you are going to Australia to speak to him, you'll never find any of this out. Mike seems to be in control when Dale is away, and is happy to help on anything you may to know. The hostel has a licence for alcohol, meaning that many, many, many

heavy nights of drunken partying take place here. There is even a very helpful job board located in the common room, with plenty of listings of local employment etc.

Dorm rooms are £14pn if you share with 4 people, or £13 if you share with 400,000 people. £60pw, £5 refundable deposit.

CAMPING SITES

Oxford Camping & Caravans Club
426 Abingdon Road, Oxford
(01865) 244088
Office open daily 9am-1am and 4pm-6pm

1.5 miles from city centre, this members club is open to any visitor (provided they pay a non-members pitch fee of £4.30), has 84 pitches that take tents, trailer tents and caravans, and provides on-site showers, toilets and laundry. Although they do take backpackers, two nights is usually the maximum stay and gangs of more than three men might find themselves turned away.

Open all year round, prices range from £3.75-£5.30 per person, per night, depending on the season.

B&B LISTINGS

Iffley Road
Acorn Guest House
260 Iffley Road (01865) 247 998
Bronte Guest House
282 Iffley Road (01865) 244 594
Brown's Guest House
281 Iffley Road (01865) 246 822
Heather House
192 Iffley Road (01865) 249 757
Isis Guest House (Summer only)
45-53 Iffley Road (01865) 248 894
Milka's Guest House
379 Iffley Road (01865) 778 458
The Balkan Lodge Hotel
315 Iffley Rd (01865) 244 524
The Palace Hotel
250-250a Iffley Rd (01865) 727 627

Banbury Road
Five Mile View Guest House
528 Banbury Road (01865) 558 747
Holly Bush Guest House
530 Banbury Road (01865) 554 886
Lonsdale Bed and Breakfast
312 Banbury Road (01865) 554 872
Ryans Guest House
164 Banbury Road (01865) 558 876
Adams Guest House
302 Banbury Road (01865) 556 118
Casa Villa Guest House
388 Banbury Road (01865) 512 642
Cotswold House
363 Banbury Road (01865) 310 558

Headington
Mulberry Guest House
265 London Road (01865) 767 114
Mount Pleasant Hotel
76 London Road (01865) 762 749
Pickwicks
5-17 London Road (01865) 750 487
Sandfield House
19 London Road (01865) 762 406

Out of Oxford

Woodstock and Blenheim Palace

(01993) 811091 Park open every day from
9am-4.45pm Palace opens 10.30am-4.45pm
Admission for park only £5 per car or £1
per person on foot
The park is open all year round, while the
palace opens mid-March to late autumn

Nothing to do with the bird in the
Peanuts cartoon or the Hippyfest,
Woodstock is actually the kind of
English village that American tourists
go weak at the knees for, and with
Blenhiem Palace on its doorstep,
makes a perfect day out.

The grounds, designed by
Capability Brown, and palace
(designed by John Varburgh), are
where Winston Churchill* was born
and are the seat of the Dukes of
Marlborough. The front door of
Blenheim Palace has the biggest lock
in the world, the enormous key of
which used to cause no end of grief
to Churchill; he would always keep it
in his right hand trouser pocket,
which is why, in photos, his trousers
always seem to hang to the right in
an alarming fashion. If you enjoy
nosing around someone else's house
the charge is a hefty £10 for adult,
and £5 for children, while, in a
separate part of the park near the
palace, you can pay another £1.50 to
run around a maze, or marvel at
other things, like their human sundial
and various puzzles.

A good way to enjoy Blenheim is
to get together a big group of friends,
a huge picnic, some booze, a Frisbee
and find a good spot to flop around,
as the park itself it quite magnificent.
Alternatively, just come for a good
long ramble around the lake, through
the woods, and over the scrubland.
For the more frugal, you can even get
in free through a public right of way
situated near The Black Prince pub at
the far end of Woodstock.

The Sculpture Park, Christmas Common

To find it take the B480 through
Stadhampton to Watlington, through the
town centre andthen take the little road
on the right up the hill to Christmas
Common. Turn left at top of hill and keep
your eyes open for a carpark on your right
(it's about ½ hour drive from Oxford and
three hours by space-hopper).
Always open and great for kids.

Perfect if you want to do something
different one Sunday afternoon. The
park has over 20 sculptures dotted
around its woodland, including mirrors
in trees, strange towers, things you can
climb on, and things you can bang.
Bring a picnic and a camera.

*For anyone interested in such things, his grave can
be found in the church graveyard in Bladdon, a
small village just before Woodstock on the right.

The Uffington White Horse & Dragon Hill

Both visible from the B4507 between Woolstone and Kingstone Lisle, just past Wantage. Parking available.

The White Horse is 'the loveliest of all British hill-figures' according to modern-day mystic Julian Cope. This 120 yard-long horse (which, arguably, looks more like a cat) dates back to 100B.C. and can be seen clearly from a lay-by. For the true English experience though, you will need to bring with you some Tupperware containing limp salmon sandwiches and a flask of tepid tea to consume whilst viewing this Neolithic marvel.

Nearby, Dragon Hill, a natural cone-shaped hill, is the legendary place where St. George killed the dragon. The chalky bald bit on top is said to be where the Dragon's blood fell and, as a consequence, no grass has grown there since.

Shotover Country Park

Just on the outskirts of Oxford up past Headington. To find it go along Old Road and up over the ring road to the top of the hill.

This vast park, a short drive from the city, offers nature walks, mountain bike trails, trees to climb, picnic areas and occasional special events such as the egg-rolling competition at Easter*.

Harcourt Arboretum

(01865) 343501
Just down the A4074, a little past Nuneham Courtenay. Open 10am-5pm May-Oct daily, 10am-4.30pm Nov-Apr (but closed Sundays) Free admission, Though there is a charge for parking So it's not really free

Close to Oxford and ideal for an afternoon jaunt to clear alcoholic cobwebs. Its winding paths through various flora and tree environments are worth visiting any time of year, except perhaps February. But, let's face it, **nothing** looks good in February.

Cotswold Wildlife Park

Burford (20 miles outside Oxford)
This walkabout park has all the classic textbook animals (lions, leopards, rhino, zebras, camels, antelopes etc), as well as a 'petting zoo' where you/your kids can fondle goats. There's also an adventure playground, a wee train, and café. Good value for all weathers and a good spot to bring children.

*See Diary of Events

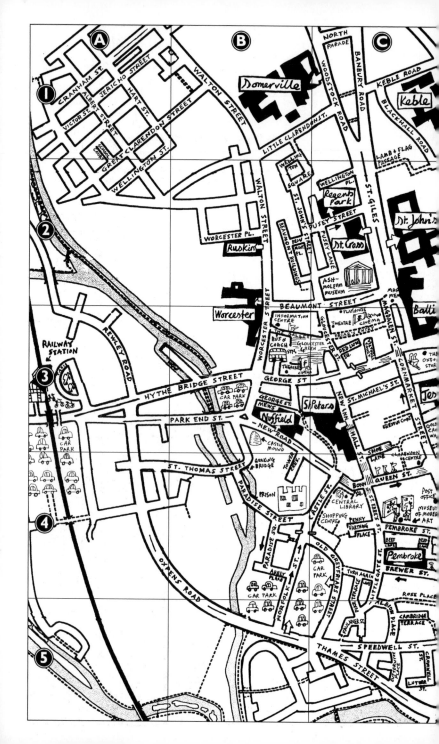

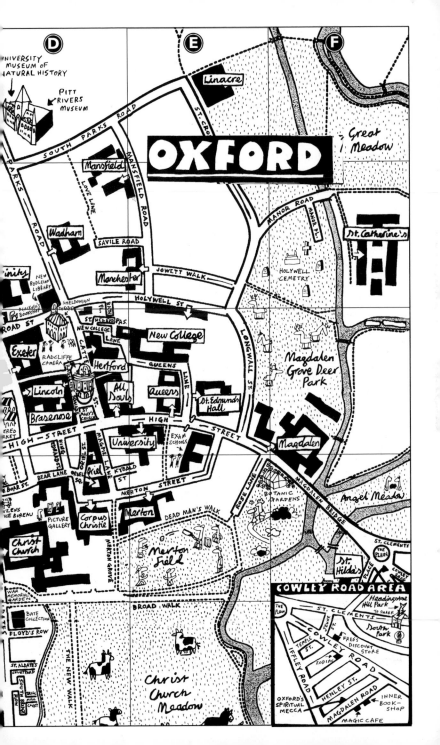

INDEX FOR MAP

A few Useful Numbers

HOSPITALS

John Radcliffe (Casualty)
Headley Way, Headington
(01865) 741166

Radcliffe Infirmary (ENT)
Woodstock Road,
(01865) 311188

Nuffield Orthopaedic
Windmill Road, Headington
(01865) 741155

Churchill
Old Road, Headington
(01865) 741841

The Acland
25 Banbury Road, Oxford
(01865) 52081

HEALTH CENTRES

Blackbird Leys Health Centre
Blackbird Leys Rd, (01865) 246388

Botley Health Unit
West Way House, Elms Parade
(01865) 246388

East Oxford Health Centre
Manzil Way (01865) 242109

North Oxford Medical Centre
96 Woodstock Road (01865) 311005

Quarry Surgery
248 London Road, Headington
(01865) 761047

South Oxford Health Centre
Lake St, (01865) 244428

St Bartholomews Medical
Manzil Way (01865) 242334

Temple Cowley Health Centre
Temple Road, Cowley
(01865) 7770294

West Oxford Health Centre
Binsey Lane (01865) 246495

ADVICE LINES

Drug & Alcohol Problems
(01865) 226243

LIFE Pregnancy Care Service
(01865) 202435

OXAIDS
(01865) 243389 advice and support on
HIV infection and AIDS

Oxford Friend
(01865) 726893 support/information for
gay and bisexuals. 7-9pm Tues, Wed and Fri.

Oxford Sexual Abuse & Rape Crisis Centre
(01865) 726295

Oxfordshire Counselling Service
(01865) 308999

Samaritans
(01865) 722122

Relate
(01865) 242960

Student Nightline
(01865) 553456 confidential listening
service for students by students.
8pm-8am (During term)

220

Also available from Cheeky:

Hilarious and irreverent, the *Cheeky Guide to Love* is a self-help manual for the bewildered twenty-first century lover. Applying the old adage - *'the course of true love never did run smooth'* - this book takes the reader through the thorny problems of: attracting a partner, falling in love with them and keeping them from running away (once you've let slip your less appealing habits). It also offers ideas on how to spice up a stag, hen and wedding night, and even how to cope with the heartache of the inevitable divorce, ten years later.

In true Cheeky Guide style, this book is packed with humour, cartoons, quizzes, games and photo love stories, and veers from the beaten path to offer advice on:

• Alternative weddings
• Dating tips for the hideously ugly
• How to bag a mail-order bride
• The best films for a romantic night in
• Coping with celibacy
• How to write a 'Mills and Boon' novel
• 'Courting' tips for the old folk
• How to reap revenge on a cheating partner

As a gift between lovers, for those about to wed, the lonely, the dumped or those beyond salvation, the Cheeky Guide to Love promises to resolve all issues of the heart, bringing joy and happiness to all who read it. And failing that, it makes a handy-sized missile to be thrown during a lovers' tiff.

Also available from Cheeky:

The Cheeky Guide to Student Life is the essential item that no student can afford to be without. The book offers a tongue in cheek insight into all aspects of student life with useful tips, anecdotes, games and advice (most of which is legal). It is a humorous but highly informative whistle-stop tour of everything the modern-day student needs to know for squeezing the best out of their time at university.

Along with chapters on accommodation, food, housing, finance and politics, the book also includes some Cheeky trademarks including a photo-love story, the weirdest places to study in the UK, how to plagiarise essays, the best male-to-female ratios for each college, stories about infamous students and lecturers, advice on how to ditch your childhood sweetheart, and what to do at the end of it all should you find yourself with a 2:2 in Philosophy and completely unemployable.

The Cheeky Guide to Student Life - ISBN: 09536110 35 - 384 Pages

A wealth of useful information and sound advice - John Clare, Daily Telegraph

Part of the fabulous Cheeky Guide series, this is a hilarious read for past, present and future students. Prepare for 'laugh-out-loud' moments! - Kickstart life.co.uk

Also available from Cheeky:

The Cheeky Guide to Brighton will take you on a factual but comic journey to the many corners of this celebrated town, taking in its famous nightlife, gay scene and exotic shops, as well as lesser-known features such as llama-trekking and where to contact the dead.

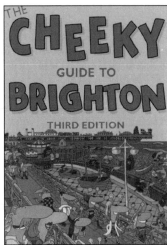

Expect a wealth of funny stories and bizarre characters, as the book dishes out such essential information as where to eat the best fish and chips, where to spot your favourite celebrity, and what to do in an emergency, should you find yourself at Brighton Marina.

This second edition comes with over 500 new entries, more cartoons and photos, four new chapters, (including the much-awaited update section on local eccentrics) and even a free 'scratch and sniff' guide to the best local restaurants.

Whether you are staying in Brighton for 3 days, 3 years or a lifetime, this book is a must.

"Captures the spirit of Brighton perfectly" - Skint Records

As featured in the Daily Telegraph, Evening Standard, The Source, Insight, and on Radio 4's Newsquiz.

The Cheeky Guide to Brighton is available nationally in all major bookshops. Online the books can be purchased via *www.amazon.com.*

Not only Brighton's best-selling guide book, but Brighton's best-selling book!